the Eaten Word

Also by Jay Jacobs

RFK: His Life and Death
A History of Gastronomy
The Color Encyclopedia of World Art
New York à la Carte
Winning the Restaurant Game
Cooking for All It's Worth
A Glutton for Punishment

the Eaten Word

THE LANGUAGE OF FOOD, THE FOOD IN OUR LANGUAGE

Jay Jacobs

A BIRCH LANE PRESS BOOK

PUBLISHED BY CAROL PUBLISHING GROUP

A Birch Lane Press Book
Published by Carol Publishing Group
Birch Lane Press is a registered trademark of Carol
Communications, Inc.
Editorial Offices: 600 Madison Avenue, New York, N.Y. 10022
Sales and Distribution Offices: 120 Enterprise Avenue, Secaucus,
N.J. 07094
In Canada: Canadian Manda Group, One Atlantic Avenue, Suite 105,
Toronto, Ontario M6K 3E7
Queries regarding rights and permissions should be addressed to Carol
Publishing Group, 600 Madison Avenue, New York, N.Y. 10022

Carol Publishing Group books are available at special discounts for bulk
purchases, sales promotion, fund-raising, or educational purposes.
Special editions can be created to specifications. For details, contact:
Special Sales Department, Carol Publishing Group, 120 Enterprise
Avenue, Secaucus, N.J. 07094

Manufactured in the United States of America
10 9 8 7 6 5 4 3 2 1

Library of Congress Cataloging-in-Publication Data
Jacobs, Jay.
    The eaten word : the language of food, the food in our language /
by Jay Jacobs.
        p. cm.
    "A Birch Lane Press Book."
    ISBN 1-55972-285-1 (hard cover)
    1. Food—Terminology. 2. Gastronomy—Terminology. 3. English
language—Terms and phrases. 4. Figures of speech. I. Title.
TX349.J33 1995   94-25237
641'.014—dc20   CIP

*For Marion Gorman, her friendship and loyalty,
and for Hope and Neal, who share her decency*

A Georgia peach, a real Georgia peach, a backyard great-grandmother's orchard peach, is as thickly furred as a sweater, and so fluent and sweet that once you bite through the flannel, it brings tears to your eyes. The voices of the coastal people were like half-wild and lovely local peaches, compared to the bald, dry, homogenous peaches displayed at a slant in the national chain supermarkets.

—Melissa Fay Greene, *Praying for Sheetrock*

Contents

The Elusive Shoemaker

Although I didn't realize it at the time, the idea behind this book began to germinate in the late 1970s and early 1980s, when my reading matter consisted in large part of restaurant menus. I was then working as a hired belly: a professional eater who earned his daily bread by gorging on rarefied delicacies, sluiced down with pedigreed wines, for a magazine whose title works out anagrammatically to "more gut." In short, I was a restaurant reviewer. Or "critic" in my more fatuous moments.

Vocationally, a relatively small group of maladjusted colleagues and I were anachronisms: living fossils, throwbacks to prehistoric times when the sole occupation of all earth's creatures, protohumans included, was the feeding of the face. True, I was paid to produce a certain amount of evaluative prose each month, but that seemed to me to be ancillary to the primary task. Writing about what I ate struck me as roughly analogous to, although it was somewhat more ephemeral, painting the cave walls of Altamira or

Lascaux with depictions of what had been, would be or was hoped to be eaten.

Such as it was, my mandate was to convey my eating experiences and reactions thereto to my readers by means of language, a notoriously unreliable vehicle for the conveyance of subjective reaction. As did others of my ilk, I muddled through as best I could, playing thimblerig with a meager stock of threadbare adjectives applied indiscriminately and meaninglessly to a whole spectrum of disparate sensory perceptions.

While I was bored numb by the necessarily limited vocabulary of food writing, I was endlessly fascinated by the nomenclature and terminology of the kitchen and the table and by the pervasive influence on language in general of culinary and gastronomic metaphors, similes and tropes. The interest originally was piqued as a matter of idle curiosity by the name of a dish then common to most Italian restaurant menus: *pollo alla scarpariello,* or "chicken shoemaker's style."

Like the various regional cuisines of Italy, Italian culinary terminology is as colorful, imaginative and exuberant as any in the Western world. If you take the Italians' nomenclatural testimony literally, you'll eat any or all of the following: trousers, muffs, bow ties, slippers, little rags, priests' hats, priest stranglers, nuns' chatter, nuns' thighs, St. Agatha's breasts and nipples of the Virgin. Those with ocular propensities consume the eyes of mothers-in-law and St. Lucia and wolves and trout. Women's sweet lies figure in some regional diets, along with ladies' mouths, old women's teeth, big ears, little fingers, mustaches, goats' and monks' beards, Moors' heads and hunchbacks. Hardware fanciers may scarf down radiators, sewer pipes, pen nibs and rifles. For those concerned with fibrous intake, there are straw and hay, little bundles, sheet music and playing cards. Italians also will tell you that they ingest little worms, rocksplitters, seashells, a thousand infantrymen and twins among a near-infinitude of options unavailable or abjured in most parts of the world.

Although the Greeks of classical antiquity had employed freelance Sicilian chefs to supervise their more elaborate gastronomic blowouts and the French nobles of the sixteenth century installed Italian *chefs de cuisine* in the kitchens of their châteaux, there never had been much of a tradition of chefly professionalism in Italy itself. Italian cooking over time had been—and largely remains today—*cucina alla casalinga*: home cooking, uncodified and idiosyncratic from region to region, village to village, even family to family within isolated hamlets.

Before and after the French Revolution, on the other hand, most of the classic French dishes, sauces and garnishes of *haute cuisine* were the products of professional, often sycophantic chefs who tended to name their creations for aristocratic patrons (Du Barry, Marie-Louise, Marigny, et al.) and for women of fashion (the otherwise unidentified Suzette of *crêpes Suzette,* for example, reputedly a mistress of the Prince of Wales during the Belle Epoque, and Anna Deslions, a member of the Second Empire glitterati, who is remembered today, glancingly, as the eponymous dedicatee of *pommes Anna,* a dish devised by Adolphe Dugléré, whose own name survives as the author of a richly sauced flatfish, as does that of his slightly later colleague, Nicolas Marguery, of whose best shot at immortality an American in Paris, Julian Street, wrote some years after the chef's demise in 1910, "His sole goes marching on"). Other French dishes honored such operatic and theatrical luminaries as Nellie Melba— a peach of a girl and the toast of three continents—or commemorated military victories (e.g., chicken Marengo, supposedly cobbled together with scrounged ingredients after Bonaparte's defeat of the Austrians in 1800, outside the village for which the improvised dish was named).

In contrast to the French professionals, Italian home cooks and the proprietors of mom-and-pop eating establishments have been notably democratic in ascribing the origins of their emblematic dishes not to the Beautiful People but to ordinary working stiffs. Italian culinary nomenclature is replete with generic blue-collar and peasant attributions—dishes supposedly prepared in the styles of woodcutters, hunters, gardeners, carters, sailors, fishermen, grandmothers, rabbis, coalmen, nuns and prostitutes, among many others. (After the arrival of Catherine de Medici in Marseilles in 1533, the French appropriated a few such designations, but never with much conviction; as long as a choice remained between fine and coarse complexions, finery and rags, authorship or inspiration was ascribed in France to the folks on the right side of the tracks.) In Italy in most cases, the folk ascriptions are plausible enough. *Spaghetti alla puttanesca,* or whore's spaghetti, for example, came by its name either because the dish was favored by Neapolitan working girls who found that it could be slapped together in minutes, between tricks, or (according to another theory) because its aroma was seductive enough to lure casual passersby into fleshly transactions.

A case can be made for either premise, and the truth may lie somewhere between the two, but neither lacks plausibility. Nor do the standard explanations of how other such dishes came by their names. It's generally agreed, for example, that *marinara* treatments were credited to sailors because their preferred meatless sauces were made with ingredients less apt to spoil at sea and more amenable to quick preparation, with minimal risk of fire aboard wooden ships. Dishes prepared *alla boscaiuolo* (woodcutter's style) or *alla cacciatore* (hunter's style) invariably contain an abundance of mushrooms, readily available to men who took their lunch breaks in the forests. Similarly, many flour-dredged dishes are cooked in the style of the miller's wife (*alla mugnaia*), who traditionally put excess flour to as many uses as she could back in the days when her husband bartered his services for a tenth part of the grain he milled.

But how did the shoemaker get into the act?

Over the years I questioned scores of Italian chefs and restaurateurs about the matter, invariably eliciting nothing but shrugs. The many cookbooks and culinary histories I consulted were equally uninformative. I had just about written off the possibility of solving the mystery when I found myself seated in still another Italian restaurant, with *pollo alla scarpariello* once more listed on the menu. Once more I put the usual—by then obsessional—question to the *padrone*, expecting once more a shrugged expression of ignorance. "Look at the dish," he said. "What do you see? Little bits of chicken on the bone, right? Today, here in America, we try to eat them with a knife and fork, but the country people back in the old days in Italy, they knew better. They ate them with their fingers."

I had to concede that the fingers (which the French term *la fourchette d'Adam,* or "Adam's fork") were eminently better suited to the job than flatware. But still, what was the shoemaker connection? "Because the dish tasted so good," the owner replied, "people ate it as fast as they could."

Okay, terrific, I conceded, but what the hell has all this folkloric argle-bargle to do with the name of the dish? "Think of a shoemaker in his shop," my man said. "How does he work? He has a mouthful of tacks and his fingers keep flying to his lips, right? And that's what you used to see in the old country when people ate *pollo alla scarpariello.* And that's how the dish got its name, right?"

Right. Indisputably, ineluctably, unarguably right.

From that moment on, I found myself speculating about every seemingly unaccountable or obscurely derived culinary or gastronomic term I came across. Why is the fish John Dory known as Saint-Pierre, San Pietro and San Pedro in France, Italy and Spain, respectively, and how, for that matter, did it come by its peculiar English handle? Why do "lettuce" and "milk" share a common etymology? Why did the British borrow the French term *dent de lion* ("lion's tooth") for "dandelion" although the French themselves more bluntly and indelicately refer to the salad green as *pissenlit* ("piss in bed"), and what have dandelions to do with bedly incontinence? Why was a certain treatment of eggplant (and why "*egg*plant"?) dubbed *melanzane alla parmigiana* when the dish originated in Sicily, had no connection with Parma and makes no use of Parmesan cheese or Parma ham? Why is the edible tuber of the sunflower *Helianthus tuberosus* called "Jerusalem artichoke" in English, when it is neither indigenous to the Old World nor a member of the artichoke family, and why did its French name, *topinambour,* which has no connection with either of the foregoing, come into currency? Why was a dish originally designated "lobster Wenberg" rechristened "lobster Newburg" in honor of neither an existing place nor a person? How did the so-called Tenderloin District of New York City, now a synonym for urban grunge, come to be identified with an eminently desirable cut of beef?

The baffling case of *melanzane alla parmigiana* wasn't cleared up for me until 1989, with the publication of *Pomp and Sustenance,* Mary Taylor Simeti's splendid, witty overview of "Twenty-five Centuries of Sicilian Food" (the book's subtitle). Simeti, a native New Yorker who settled in Sicily the better part of three decades ago, explains the seemingly anomalous term this way: "Sicilians have a word, *palmigiana,* that means 'shutter' and that stems from the overlapping louvers of a shutter and the overlapping palm fronds in a thatched roof. Someone was reminded of a shutter as he covered a pan of overlapping eggplant slices and caciocavallo, hence *melanzane alla palmigiana.* Since Sicilians have a 'probrem' pronouncing the *l,* confusion was sure to follow."

Except for the two questions already resolved, all the foregoing and a great many other puzzlers that pepper the language of food will be dealt with in the pages to come, as will many of the countless food-derived figures of speech that permeate human discourse, written, oral and pictorial, and that are in large part used unconsciously in ordinary conversation, formal writing and the visual arts. Why, after working to "put bread on the table," do we "bring home the bacon" instead? What was the original, literal meaning of "apple of one's eye"? What, exactly, is "humble pie," and should we really be embarrassed to eat it? How does the expression "making ends meet" relate to Elizabethan table etiquette?

Since the dawn of history, societies have propitiated their gods or ruling spirits with ritual offerings of food (e.g., the dishes and seeds buried with the pharoahs, the Homeric burnt offerings, the Passover matzoh, the bread and wine of the Eucharist, the paschal lamb and eggs) and have made their staple foods of choice synonymous with their specie and paper currency ("bread," "cabbage," "beans," "kale," "clams," etc.). In many Old and New World societies, rice is thrown at newlyweds, spilt salt is thrown over the left shoulder and leguminous seeds—lentils in much of Europe, black-eyed peas (in conjunction with collard greens) in Dixie—are eaten at the New Year to ensure prosperity during the coming months. In post-Colonial domestic architecture of the Federal period, the pineapple was a recurrent motif, symbolic of hospitality. In certain African cultures, as Margaret Visser notes in her book *The Rituals of Dinner,* to accept a proffered bowl of food with only one hand is a serious breach of etiquette, as is an Arab host's failure to pour your tea until an excess of the beverage slops over into the saucer or a German guest's failure to mop up every last trace of food on the plate. All these ritual usages and hundreds more traditionally have inflected symbolic languages whose messages were clearly apprehensible to, and strictly observed by, their initiates but in many cases have been obscured with the passage of time, to be replaced by the verbal and nonverbal vocabularies and syntax of succeeding generations, the origins of whose coded messages doubtless will become equally obscure as time rolls by.

Why do Roman Catholics place a sprig of rosemary in the font after a death in the family, and why were grooms traditionally presented with sprigs of the same herb by bridesmaids on the wedding day? Why do Italian growers of their indispensable herb, basil, believe that it thrives best when cussed out roundly and regularly, and what has their name for it to do with royalty, certain churches and a legendary dragon with lethal breath and glance? Why do various Inuit cultures of the Arctic and its environs resent the now politically incorrect, diet-derived term "Eskimo" as an aspersion on their eating habits, and what are the underlying bases for such analogous ethnic slurs as "frogs," "krauts," *"mangiafagioli,"* "spaghetti benders" and the Japanese "butter-stinkers," that last applied to Caucasians of any stripe?

Questions, questions. Let's hope the answers to most will materialize in the forthcoming pages, along with some informed speculation about the others.

Part 1

CHAPTER 1

Wording Our Eats

The human mouth—an early prototype of the food processor and various electronic communications devices—is an extraordinary mechanism. The conduit for both alimentation and primary social intercourse (and, to a lesser extent, respiration and amatory interaction), its two chief functions have been linked inextricably since the first grunt of satisfaction with a handful of nuts or berries or grubs opened the way for the natterings of today's food writers and restaurant critics.

Of all the bodily appendages or organs, only the mouth, alone or collaboratively, is the receptor or transmitter of four of the five senses. While the eye, ear, nose and palate surfaces have only a single sensory function apiece (although the nose assists in the apprehension of flavor), the functions of the mouth are brought to bear, in varying circumstances and to greater or lesser degrees, on every sense save sight.

Within our individual lifetimes and collectively as a species, we

humans ate before we spoke. Throughout all but a relatively infin-
itesimal recent phase of its development, humankind made a full-
time job of feeding itself (as all other living creatures did and still
do, except in a few rare cases in which human intervention has
altered behavior).

Given such a state of affairs, it was inevitable that once our remote
ancestors acquired a rudimentary gift of gab, their chief, if not sole,
topic of conversation would have been the quest for, and preparation
and consumption of, their daily provender; when any society's
sphere of interest effectively is limited to a single function and its
closely related activities, communicative options and the development of an extended vocabulary and syntax are restricted accordingly. In all likelihood, the earliest spoken languages consisted of
little or nothing beyond food nomenclature, common nouns for a
few food-related implements and a scattering of verbs having to do
in one fundamental way or another with food procurement and
preparation. Thus, the Neanderthal homemaker we'll call Yurp
probably didn't encourage her mate, Ugh, to have a nice day at the
office and pick up a copy of *TV Guide* on the way home but more
likely urged him to "Go, kill eats."

Today, countless millennia and innumerable technological and
linguistic advances later, metaphors, imagery, symbolism and various tropes—derived from what we eat, how we prepare it and what
our attitudes toward it may be, many of them invoked without
conscious recognition of their sources—are common elements of
our daily speech and our literature. When we resort to the adjective
"mellifluous," for example (if any of us still do), few of us con-

sciously realize that its Latin roots combine the noun *mel* ("honey") with the verb *fluus* ("to flow [like]"), although we may more readily recognize "honeyed tones" as a food-derived figure of speech.

Sixty-odd years ago, three Babylonian cuneiform tablets, compiled or stenographically recorded by an unknown scribe between 1792 and 1750 B.C., probably during the reign of Hammurabi, were unearthed in what is now Iraq. The tablets languished in obscurity in Yale University's Babylonian Collection until quite recently, when a prominent French Assyriologist, avocational cook and celebrated Parisian gourmand, Jean Bottéro, recognized them for what they were: the world's oldest cookbooks, predating that distinction's previous claimant, a collection of Roman recipes supposedly compiled in the first century of the Christian era, by a millennium and three-quarters.

The still-legible portions of the Assyrian texts, now gradually being translated, comprise upward of thirty relatively systematic recipes. Translation of the whole corpus is progressing slowly, possibly because Professor Bottéro's scholarly dedication has been compromised to some extent by his typically Gallic epicurean sensibilities: of the Babylonian recipes, he has written that he "wouldn't wish such meals [on his] worst enemies."

Of those transcriptions that have been conditionally rendered, one is for a stew featuring a domestic fowl of undetermined species. In the recipe the bird is termed *kippu*, and we're told that it should be prepared "as you would agarukku," another as-yet-unidentified species of domestic poultry. My own speculation is that both *kippu* and *agarukku* may have been onomatopoeic renderings of the cries of the domestic hen and cock, respectively, or some such prototypes thereof, but there ain't nobody here but them long-defunct chickens to conclusively confirm or deny a wild stab. (Onomatopoeia, the formation of words from their sound referents, has played a somewhat ambiguous role in the language of food and will be dealt with a bit later in this chapter.)

The origins of the earliest nouns applied to foodstuffs are as obscure as those of language in general. The etymology of most terms now in use can be traced to ancient roots, but we're ultimately stopped cold by an impenetrable wall erected sometime before the onset of traceable documentation—a wall that divides linguistic prehistory from the earliest known sources of terms still in common use. We know, for example, that "butter" and such cognates as the French *beurre* and Italian *burro* are descended from the Greek *bouturen* ("cow cheese"), but the identity of the seed from which the root form derived is simply unknowable at this distant remove.

Nor is it necessary to delve very far back into history to find ourselves on slippery etymological ground. The origins of such post-Colonial American terms as "anadama bread," "johnnycakes" and "hush puppies" have yet to be resolved to general satisfaction among those who care about such matters, and debate still drags on among French nitpickers about whether a dish originated around 1860 properly should be termed lobster *à l'américaine* or *à l'armoricaine*. (Before the invasion of northwestern France by fifth-century Britons, what is now Brittany was known as Armorica.) Despite considerable evidence to the contrary, including hearsay testimony by the legendary French gourmand Curnonsky (Maurice Edmond

Sailland, 1872–1956), who contended that the dish was indisputably the creation of a chef who had changed his name from Fraisse to Peters while working in the United States during the 1850s, the more intransigently chauvinistic of Curnonsky's compatriots still insist that the birthplace of the dish had to be Armorica, not America. As it happened, the nativity actually occurred in Paris, where the repatriated Peters had opened a restaurant around 1860, and where he cobbled up an improvisatory dish one night for an unexpected party of after-hours drop-ins. Pressed to identify his spur-of-the-moment creation by name, Peters, memories of his New World sojourn still fresh in his mind, blurted, *"Homard à l'américaine."*

Such was the story as reported to Curnonsky many years later by another Parisian restaurateur named Garrigue, who had known Peters many years before *then* and claimed to have received it straight from the horse's mouth. It has a ring of truth about it that the Armorican attribution—on its face a product of wishful patriotic thinking—lacks. Wishful thinking, whether motivated by anecdotal plausibility, superficial linguistic credibility or folkloric suasion, has made one hell of a muddle of the genesis and evolution of a great many food-related terms in various languages.

To examine a few such terms prominent in ordinary speech, let's start with that which, after "bread," is probably in most frequent use, whether in literal application or as a metaphor in the Western world: "apple." Although Genesis tells us only that Eve "ate of the tree which is in the middle of the garden," elsewhere identified as

"the tree of the knowledge of good and evil," conventional wisdom
and the iconology of the visual arts almost from the get-go have
specified the apple as the agent of temptation and ruin—and nonetheless of almost all that has been beneficent in the world once the
first couple were eighty-sixed from the Garden (more on that in the
next chapter).

An otherwise generally reliable book on food lore published in
1991 confidently asserts that the noun we're concerned with here
"comes from a province of Italy called Abela, where the modern
apple is thought to have first appeared." The assertion is immediately suspect: not only is there no such province in Italy as Abela,
there are no provinces in Italy at all. (The official Italian designation
for a national subdivision is *regione*, not *provincia.*) Moreover, "apple" is known to have entered the English language (via the Teutonic *applen*) sometime before the late ninth century, a time when
Britons had not, by some years (roughly a millennium), begun to
decorate their cultural baggage with Grand Tour travel stickers or
even heard of the notional Italian province.

How the early Teutons may have come by their *applen*, and their
northern European contemporaries by *their* various close cognates
thereof, is one of those linguistic mysteries that even the relentless
Oxford English Dictionary (henceforth OED) dismisses with a
shrug, as most dictionaries and etymologists dismiss speculation
about the earliest word forms, other than the few that are clearly
onomatopoeic in origin. (The nearest thing to a homophone for
"Abela" in English, incidentally, is "abele," the white poplar, derived from the Latin *albus* [white], whence also "albino.")

Let's assume now that you've avoided commercially standardized, zombie-"ripened" produce and hold in your hand a fragrantly luscious apricot. How did the fruit come by its name? Along with many other fruits and vegetables, it derives its common name from the characteristics of its growth. Originally "abrecock" in English, the term can be traced through various permutations in several languages to the Latin (*prunum*) *praecoquum*, the precocious plum, a fruit that ripened earlier than the true plum or any of its standard cousins.

The etymology of "artichoke" is so confused that the OED finds itself more or less at a loss for words in attempting to track it with any precision to its probable Arabic source. Like the apricot, the artichoke was cockier at one point in its linguistic evolution (when "archecocks" were brought "to the king's grace" in 1531) than it is today. (The king's grace was superseded by the queen's—the first Elizabeth's—two years later. Unlike another, still later national leader, U.S. president George Bush, whose aversion to broccoli became a matter of public record, Bess was noncommittal about her veggies.) The prevailing opinion among those who bother their heads about such matters is that the term originated in Arabic as *al-kharshūf*, but how or why is anybody's guess.

However obscure the origins of "artichoke" may be, the genesis of "Jerusalem artichoke" (neither indigenous to the Holy Land nor botanically related to the true artichoke) is no great mystery. The Jerusalem artichoke is the edible tuberous root of the New World sunflower *Helianthus tuberosus*. Sunflowers of other species had been cultivated in the Old World for the oil extracted from their seeds long before the discovery and importation of *H. tuberosus.* The Italians had dubbed *their* sunflower *girasole,* from *girare,* "to turn," and *sole,* "sun," with "toward" implied between the verb and noun, as had the Spanish, who omitted the terminal *e,* while the French *tournesol* had the same meaning. At some indeterminate point the Italian term found its way into English (where it survives today as a synonym for the fire opal). Sir Philip Sidney, the Elizabethan courtier and poet, used it in 1586, when he wrote, "With gazing looks, short sighes, unsettled feet he stood, but turned, as Girosol, to sun." By then, however, Sidney was making use of a fast-fading archaism, for "sonne flower" had entered the language no later than 1562, and probably a good deal earlier.

A widely perceived similarity between the flavor of the naturalized American tuber and that of the true artichoke (the edible flower of the plant *Cynara scolymus*) had led to "girasole artichoke," but as *girasole* faded into obsolescence in English it was replaced by the vaguely homonymous, altogether irrelevant "Jerusalem." As one English observer remarked in the early 1860s, "From this *girasol* we have made Jerusalem, and from the Jerusalem artichoke we make Palestine soup."

The notional cachet conferred on the tuber by its supposed link to the Holy Land wasn't lost in those parts of Britain where the tuber also was known as the "Jerusalem potato." As often has been the case with English food terminology, nouns derived from foreign sources have been adapted as like-sounding terms with more rhyme than reason. And if the garbled result was invested with an aura of sanctity, so much the better.

The herb rosemary, for example, which will be dealt with in another context later on, originally was named, like the sunflower, for a growth characteristic but took on religious overtones in Medieval England, when the Latin *rose* ("dew") and *marinus* ("of the sea") became "rose of Mary." The Romans of classical antiquity had named the shrub, which grew best along mist-shrouded shores, in an eminently pragmatic manner. The more mystically inclined Brits of the Middle Ages, however, cobbled up a legend whereby the shrub's blossoms, previously white, came by their blue tint when the Virgin Mary, fleeing from Herod's soldiers into Egypt with the infant Jesus in her care, draped her blue cloak overnight on a *rosmarinus* bush. The question of why Mary might have doffed the garment during the chill hours between dusk and dawn, after wearing it all day under a punishing desert sun, was skirted by theologians and botanists alike. *Rosmarinus* (still *rosmarino* in Italian and *romarin* in French today) became "rose of Mary" in English, later elided to "rosemary."

To return for a moment to the Jerusalem artichoke, just about the only vestigial memories of both France's colonial aspirations in South America and an indigenous Brazilian people survive in the modern French noun for the tuber: *topinambour.* In 1555 the French established an outpost of empire at what later was to become Rio de Janeiro but were driven out by the Portuguese a dozen years later. A second French beachhead was landed in 1612, on the island of Maranhão, but the Portuguese once again kicked French butt, and France's dreams of glory in the Southern Hemisphere were dead in the water about a thousand days after the landing. During their

abortive expansionist drive, however, the French had been introduced to *Helianthus tuberosus* by Topinambou Indians, who weren't
precisely claimants to an exclusive franchise on an edible root that
had been cultivated in various parts of the Western Hemisphere for
centuries. In the nomenclature of food, however, as in other spheres
of human activity, it's often not what you know but whom you
know that counts. The would-be French colonists in South America
may not have known much botany, but they knew the Topinambou. Hence *topinambour.*

Confronted with a cornucopia of previously unimagined foodstuffs,
the colonists of the Americas often named the edibles they found
there according to the shakiest notions of their provenance, characteristics, botanical features and native terminology. From the very
outset, with Columbus's first landfall in the Western Hemisphere,
misperceptions abounded and nomenclature of every sort was capricious, to put it mildly. In quest of Asian spices Columbus fell
half a world shy of his destination, mistook a Caribbean island for
the "Indies," misnamed its inhabitants accordingly and confused
the native sweet potato (*Ipomoea batatas*) with the unrelated African
tuber of the genus *Dioscoria,* whose common English name, "yam,"
derives from the Portuguese adjective *inhame*—"edible."

   The staple cereal grain of Central America and Mexico, *Zea mays,*
its kernels still ground for the basic bread flour of those regions and
gnawed off the cob as a high-summer treat in the United States,
willy-nilly was dubbed "corn" in English, in which language the

noun had served as a generic term for any cereal grain since the Middle Ages.

The true potato, *Solanum tuberosum,* originally cultivated in the Peruvian highlands (where corn—i.e., maize—couldn't be grown), has been tagged with some curious, often altogether misguided labels in various languages. It takes its conventional name from the Taino *batata* and remains *patata* in both Spanish and Italian today, but it became "earth apple" (*pomme de terre*) in French and the vernacular "bog apple" in Ireland, and it was confused with the truffle in Germany. Originally termed "Virginia potato" in England, it was unknown in Virginia in 1586, when the first shipment arrived in Blighty. The misattribution arose when an English ship carrying produce from the coast of Colombia stopped at Virginia on the way home, to repatriate a few starving settlers. Ironically the "Virginia potato" didn't find its way to the eponymous colony until sometime after emigrés from Ulster planted it around Londonderry, Vermont, in 1719. When the so-called Virginia potato at last reached its putative home turf some years thereafter, it was rechristened "Irish potato," with its original cultivators, the Andean Inca, once again denied the credit that was their due.

"Spud," the common English colloquial term for the potato, incidentally, derives from *spudding* growing things from the soil with a *spud*: a spadelike tool originally made by hammering flat a spike-shaped iron dagger (Middle English *spuddle*) and attaching it to a plow staff. Thus, in word and deed, early British harvesters fulfilled a biblical prophecy by beating their "swords" into plowshares.

The French potato, *pomme de terre*, traces its way back to *pōmum*, a Latin noun of uncertain specific application that survives in English as "pome," the botanist's generic term for nondrupaceous fleshy fruits, which is to say stoneless or pitless varieties such as apples, pears and quinces. "Pomade," originally an apple-scented hair dressing, springs from the same root, as do the originally apple-shaped sachet "pomander"; "pomace," the pulpy residue of wine grapes and other fruits pressed for their juices or oils; *pomodoro*, the Italian for "tomato"; the French *pampelmousse* ("grapefruit") and the English "pomegranate" and "pomelo," among others.

As the commonest of European pomes, the apple usually has taken the heat or credit whenever fruit of any kind has been invoked metaphorically in any context. In Greek mythology, Eris, the personification of discord, tossed a golden apple among a gathering of the gods, who contended for its possession in most ungodly fashion. Although the forbidden fruit of Genesis is identified with no specificity, folklore has hung the rap on the apple. What is representatively defined by the American Heritage Dictionary as "the projection of the largest laryngeal cartilage at the front of the throat, especially in men" is, of course, the Adam's apple, supposedly stuck in the sinner's gullet eons before Heimlich came along to devise the simple maneuver that might have dislodged it.

The "apple of the eye" goes back to the early Middle Ages in England, when the ocular pupil was mistaken for a globular solid. The term was later extended to the iris as well and still later to the whole eyeball; it now survives as a metaphor for something or someone cherished above all others. The orb of British royal regalia is the "golden apple"; the equine turds dropped on highways and byways before the ascendency of the automobile were termed "horse apples" in this country, where "apple-knocker" was synonymous with "rube" or "hick," "yokel" or "shit-kicker," at a time when any small-town woman of dubious morality and ample endowment was known as "Apple Annie." (Much earlier, in England, an "apple squire" was a pimp.)

As a verb, "apple" survives vestigially among a few fruit harvesters and windfall gatherers, but in its earlier senses "to apple" was to bear fruit of any kind, apples included, or to form mature vegetables. As one late eighteenth-century treatise on gardening noted, "The cabbage turnep [kohlrabi] is of two kinds; one apples above ground."

And how d'ya like them apples?

After the potato, the tomato ultimately would turn out to be the Americas' most important contribution to the European table, although neither gained immediate widespread acceptance. In English, French and Spanish the tomato's common name derives nearly intact from the *tomatl* of the Nahuatl-speaking peoples subjugated by the conquistadores. The Italians, possibly in ignorance of conversational Nahuatl, had ideas of their own and named the fruit of the vine *Lypersicon esculentum* for its shape, color and lack of a central pit or stone. As it remains today (despite a few experiments in cubism by genetic engineers obsessed with the economics of shipping and handling), the tomato's original shape was roughly apple-round, with the generous convexities usually attributed to apples.

Its color at that time was yellow (as a few atavistic, ultrachic and concomitantly pricey strains are today, after generations of more or less unrelieved, intensively developed, highly appetizing redness). In view of its form, color and general resemblance to other nondrupaceous fruits, the tomato was called *pomodoro,* or "fruit of gold," by the Italians, who were among the first belatedly to recognize its culinary virtues.

Unlike the French language, Italian has a specific pomeless noun for the apple: *melo.* And while the Italians drew a clear distinction between apples and pomes in general, the French settled definitively on *pomme* as the designation for "apple." Always quick to draw amorous inferences from the blandest of constructs, they heard *pomodoro* as *pomme d'amour,* or "apple of love," which found its way into English sometime before 1579, when it was observed that "There be two kinds of Amorous or Raging love apples." Not tonight, waiter; I've got a headache.

As they did in the case of the tomato, the Spaniards introduced a wealth of previously unknown, and therefore nameless, foods into Europe. Along with the *patata* and *tomate,* several others retained their pre-Columbian names, or reasonable approximations thereof, in Spain. The Aztec *xocolatl* (literally "bitter water," the unsweetened beverage of choice of Moctezuma and his priesthood), for example, entered Spanish as *chocolate.* Similarly, the Spanish *aguacate* ("avocado") is the offspring of the Nahuatl *ahuactl* ("testicle," for the shape of the fruit), while *guava* and *papaya* both are derived from their Carib names. In many cases, these Spanish borrowings from New World languages readily were admitted into other European vocabularies (*chocolate*, for one, passed intact into English, lost its terminal vowel in French and retained most of its pronunciation, if not its orthography, in the Italian *cioccolata*), but both the Italians and the French remained resistant to *tomate*, which found its way into English about a decade before the defeat of the Spanish armada in 1588. The French finally accepted the term somewhat later, after their dalliance with the apple of love, thereby providing themselves with the option, if they chose to avail themselves of it, of dropping into a neighborhood cafe (nonexistent in the sixteenth century) and ordering a BLT (*bacon, laitue* and *tomate*) on toast. As it happened, they had—or thought they had—better things to eat, and when in the mood for casual fare they were more apt to wolf down a *croque-monsieur*: a grilled ham-and-cheese sandwich.

Since it has just, so to speak, raised its head, how did this *laitue*—and our own "lettuce," along with the Italian *lattuga* and the Spanish *lechuga*, among other cognates, come by *its* name? The various lettuces belong to the genus *Lactuca*, rooted in *lact*, the Latin for "milk." The French etymological connection between *lait* ("milk") and *laitue* ("lettuce") is more evident than the link between milk and lettuce in English, but a link exists nonetheless. While the Old English *milc* and *meolc* obviously weren't derived from Latin, the Middle English *letuse* slipped into the language via a Latinate Old French form.

But what has milk to do with all this linguistic argle-bargle? Milk is milk and lettuce is lettuce—right? Well, as many a weekend kitchen gardener ruefully has discovered, lettuce allowed to bolt, or go to seed, oozes a milky secretion that doesn't do much for a BLT or a Caesar salad, which latter, incidentally, takes its name from Caesar Cardini, the owner during the 1920s of an Italian restaurant in Tijuana, Mexico, where the dish was created. For reasons now unclear, Caesar Cardini's namesake dish originally was dubbed "aviator's salad" by its author, his brother Alex, but the *padrone* had the foresight to rechristen it in his own honor, thereby conferring a modicum of immortality on himself.

Other culinary eponyms haven't fared as well. For example, the gazeteers and biographical dictionaries I've consulted list neither a place called Newburg (although there is a Newburgh some miles up the Hudson from New York City) nor anyone of that name. How, then, did lobster Newburg land on the menus of all those restaurants that featured the dish until a generation of health-conscious diners concluded that grossly excessive intake of butter, cream and egg yolks might produce drastic clothing shrinkage and complete arterial gridlock?

Charles Ranhofer was a third-generation French chef who tyrannized his *brigade de cuisine* while kowtowing obsequiously to those clients whose "whimsicalities of taste" demanded dishes "which fill the sensitive chef's heart with despair." Ben Wenberg was a shipping executive and a regular patron of Delmonico's, the preeminent American citadel of French *haute cuisine* during the Belle Epoque, thanks largely to Ranhofer's culinary and organizational genius. Wenberg strolled into the restaurant on one occasion and presented the chef with a recipe for a murderously rich dish he had discovered—or so he claimed—during a business trip in South

America. Ranhofer's mind was blown straight through his *toque blanche*. To give the production a personal touch, he gussied up its cholesterol-charged sauce with even more egg yolks than the over-generous original recipe had called for. It appeared on the menu for the first time as "lobster Wenberg." And so it remained, a *spécialité de la maison*, at least until the dedicatee, perhaps having partaken a bit too freely of Delmonico's superb wines, got into a brawl in the dining room. He was permanently barred from the restaurant, as was his name from the menu, but the dish itself remained a popular favorite after a near-anagrammatical adjustment whereby "Wenberg" became "Newburg."

Do people who speak different languages hear nonverbal sounds differently? Sometimes it seems so. As a case in point, the English-speaking world hears—or has convinced itself that it hears—the cry of the domestic rooster as "cock-a-doodle-do," while the French and Italians hear *cocorico* and the Germans *kikeriki*. It's not altogether inconceivable that barnyard fowl, like humans, have their own regional dialects, but can kettles of simmering broth express themselves differently depending on where their contents are being cooked? The consensus among word genealogists is that "simmer" is onomatopoeic: imitative of the sound produced when liquids are heated to just below the boiling point. (As I write there's a pot of water simmering on the stove. The sound *I* hear is something vaguely susurrant, like *prrrrss*. The sound the Japanese hear is *shabu-shabu*, the name of a pot of simmering broth into which diners dunk, for cooking, thinly sliced morsels of food.)

In one phonetically almost identical form or another the term *cous-cous* is common to much of North Africa, Sicily and, since the French colonization of Algeria, France. Although there hasn't been universal agreement about the essential makeup of preparations that go by that name, the meaning of the name itself has been the subject of even more spirited debate since the first half of the nineteenth century, when the Arabic *kouskous* was orthographically modified by the French, who harbor an aversion toward the letter *k*. According to whichever garble of etymologists you choose to believe, the noun originally denoted either the duplex vessel in which the dish was cooked, the beakful of food carried to the nest by a parent bird or the pulverization of any substance, edible or not. Still another contingent of deep thinkers holds that the word, like "simmer" and *shabu-shabu*, is simply imitative of the sound produced by the cooking process itself. The imitative English word for the same sound is "hiss," which leads one to wonder whether transplanted Arabic-speaking theater-goers might have kouskoused the villains of Victorian melodramas.

One dish indisputably named for its effect on the ear as it cooks (the dish, not the ear) is the "bubble and squeak" of England. A late nineteenth-century versifier described its audible effect this way:

> What mortals Bubble call and Squeak
> When midst the frying-pan in accents savage,
> The Beef so surly quarrels with the Cabbage.

Leaving aside the question of what those mortals were doing in the frying pan, what if the dish had been invented in Italy? Is it possible that Italian ears could have heard those argumentative sounds from the skillet as *rumore di liquido che bolle e squittio?*

The *croque-monsieur* mentioned earlier, along with a number of other relatively friable French culinary preparations and the adoptive English-language "croquette," all are rooted in the verb *croquer,* "to crunch," also imitative of nonverbal sound. French dishes derived in name from the same source include the vitreously glazed, elaborately arranged pastry called *croquembouche* (which translates as "crack in the mouth"); *croquet* (no apparent connection with the lawn game), a crisp, dry cookie; *croquante,* another highly frangible production on the order of *croquembouche*; vegetables served *à la croque au sel* (crisply raw with salt); and a crackly petit four called *croquignole.* It would be inadvisable to order a *croque-monsieur* where only English is spoken; it might be heard as "Drop dead, mister."

> *Your cook has committed felony on the person of that John Dory; which is mangled in a cruel manner.*
>
> —Tobias Smollett, *Humphrey Clinker*

Smollett (1721–71) hasn't been on anyone's best-seller list lately, and, taken out of context, the quoted passage might leave most American baby boomers wondering who the unfortunate Mr. Dory was and what he had done to incur the cook's wrath. The John Dory in question is a slippery customer who not only has a slippery namesake in the New World but operates under several aliases in Europe: *San Pietro* in Italy, *Saint-Pierre* in France, *San Pedro* in

Spain, *Zeus faber* in European scientific circles and *Zenopsis ocellata* in the Western Hemisphere. Relatively few Americans have encountered him, but most of those who've crossed his path have found him a menacing presence—aggressively prognathous and dangerously armed. Europeans, on the other hand, view him as saintly and—in the hands of more compassionate cooks than Smollett's—delectable.

How the fish came by his English name is somewhat uncertain; for some three centuries before the "John" was appended to his surname he was known simply as *dorée* (French for "gilded"), or "dory" in the Anglicized form. *Dorée* is a reasonably apt description of a silvery critter with glints of gold in its hide, as is the French *daurade* for the gilt-head bream, but a minority view advancing the theory that "John" derives from *jaune*, the French for "yellow," just doesn't wash: add "yellow" to "gilded" and you have a tautology that wouldn't have passed muster (or cut the mustard) even among the groundlings in the England of Shakespeare, Marlowe and Ben Jonson. "Doubtless a humorous formation," concludes the OED, "possibly suggested by 'a very popular old song or catch' printed in 1609 . . . the subject of which is the career of John Dory, captain of a French privateer."

Johnny sports a dark spot, or ocellus, more or less amidships on either side of his laterally flattened, spiny-finned body: according to legend, the fingerprints left by St. Peter as he grasped the fish before throwing it back into the sea. A pretty story, except that our piscatorial hero is a marine denizen and the Sea of Galilee is a freshwater body (or, in today's parlance, "sodium-free"). Still another theory of the origin of the term was advanced (but is now dismissed out of hand by the OED) by the Victorian philologist E. S. Dallas (of whom we'll hear more later), who posited with flat-out certitude that "John Dory" derived from St. Peter's office as keeper of the Pearly Gates and is nothing but a corruption of the Italian *ianatore*, or "doorkeeper." Our own modern "janitor," now being phased out of use in favor of the euphemistic "maintenance engineer," once was applied only to a doorman, and one of the earliest published uses of the term in English (1686) refers to "St. Peter, reputed to be the Ianitor of Heaven." Perhaps it's John Dory who should be summoned when an apartment dweller's kitchen sink is on the fritz.

Until the Swedish botanist Carolus Linnaeus (1707–78) devised his system of taxonomic classification, the naming of foods eaten around northwestern Europe was a catch-as-catch-can business left largely in the hands of illiterate peasants, fishermen and hunters. In the course of European trade during the Middle Ages, nouns for foodstuffs shipped from one country to another often were adopted into the importers' languages. The immigrant terms usually underwent some alteration as they were naturalized, in an attempt to bring them into some sort of conformity with the adoptive language, but the orthography of the times was highly erratic, and even the spelling of native terms and proper nouns was glaringly inconsistent.

Between around 1150 and the end of the 1400s, Middle Dutch was spoken in the Netherlands, where any of various types of flat-fishes were termed *butte* (which seems, contradictorily, to have derived from Germanic or Norse roots having to do with thickness). At some undetermined point, the word found its way into England, and for reasons that remain unclear several of the larger fishes of the genus *Hippoglossus* became the holy day fare of choice. Hence, today's "halibut" evolved from a portmanteau splicing of the Old English *haligdom* ("holy") onto the Middle Dutch *butte*. As we soon shall see, the nomenclature of seafoods in general always has been somewhat capricious.

> A street there is in Paris famous,
>> For which no rhyme our language yields,
> Rue Neuve des Petits Champs its name is—
>> The New Street of the Little Fields.
> And here's an inn, not rich and splendid,
>> But still in comfortable case;
> To which in youth I oft attended,
>> To eat a bowl of Bouillabaisse.

> This Bouillabaisse a noble dish is—
>> A sort of soup, or broth, or brew,
> Or hotchpotch of all sorts of fishes,
>> That Greenwich never could outdo:
> Green herbs, red peppers, mussels, saffron,
>> Soles, onions, garlic, roach, and dace:
> All these you eat at Terre's tavern
>> In that one dish of Bouillabaisse.

Thus did William Makepeace Thackeray (who once compared eating an American oyster to "swallowing a baby") hymn the praises of one of France's emblematic regional dishes. Despite his middle name, Thackeray's verses would have made little peace in Marseilles, where proprietary rights to one of the glories of world gastronomy have been loudly proclaimed for centuries, since the Phoenicians, and then the Greeks, brought their basic fish stews to the Old Port, and where contempt has been boundless for the supposedly bastardized knockoffs served in Parisian restaurants.

Bouillabaisse takes its name from the verbs *bouiller* ("to boil") and *abaisser* ("to reduce"), which together roughly describe the cooking process involved. In its earliest Provençal readings, the dish was a mainstay of frugal coastal fisherman who cobbled up their own meals from an assortment of the unmarketable fish that turned up in their nets. *Rascasse*, for example, a singularly ugly customer much like the despised sculpin of the American Atlantic coast, is rarely eaten in any other form but is still considered *the* essential ingredient of an authentic bouillabaisse, whatever else the cook may choose to toss into the kettle.

From Thackeray's itemization of what he ate on Rue Neuve des Petits Champs, any right-minded Marseillais would conclude that he had been suckered into one of the more egregious Parisian tourist traps of his day. Both dace and roach are freshwater fish that have no place in a bona fide bouillabaisse, however divided opinion may be otherwise on the "authentic" treatment. The matter of the inclusion of mussels is less clear-cut and has been debated for generations. Although it's highly doubtful that fishing boats could have brought mussels to port, beach-bound kinfolk or neighbors may have added shallow-water contributions to the pot when the boats came home. As an example of the confusion that has clouded the issue over the years, the latest edition of *Larousse Gastronomique*, the supreme arbiter in such matters, not only condones but specifies the inclusion of mussels, while the previous edition unequivocally proscribed them: "No mussels or any other such mollusks should be added . . . as is the wont of many Paris restaurants."

Whether or not gastronomic and linguistic purists would have applied the name "bouillabaisse" to Thackeray's "hotchpotch" (a sixteenth-century culinary term derived from obscure Dutch origins via thirteenth-century English legalese, and the progenitor of today's "hodgepodge"), it must have been a fine kettle of fish. Curiously, another piscatorial French stew, *matelote*, is made with freshwater fish in most versions, although it was originally termed *plat de matelot*, or "sailor's plate." Go figure.

No fish or shellfish soup or stew originated in the United States has attained the international cachet of bouillabaisse, but a first-rate chowder, cioppino, seafood gumbo or she-crab soup is no mean production. As just about any cookbook or culinary history you choose to dip into is quick to point out, "chowder" derives from *chaudière* ("cauldron"), an Old English outgrowth of the Latin *caldarius* ("suitable for warming"). Although "cauldron" itself goes back at least to the turn of the fourteenth century in English, "chowder" didn't come into the language until the late seventeenth century, when English-speaking Canadian and Colonial American

fishermen on the Grand Banks discovered that their Breton counterparts cooked *their* version of fish stew in a *chaudière*.

Cioppino, the San Francisco fish stew, is a bit more problematic.
Although it is virtually certain that the dish was originated by immigrant Italian fishermen (isolated claims on behalf of Portuguese
San Franciscans notwithstanding), there is less certainty about the
word itself. As traditionally has been the case with communal sailors'
stews all over the world, all hands were expected to contribute to
the pot—a custom that gave rise to the somewhat shaky folk theory
that "cioppino" was a garbled rendition of "chip in." A bit more
plausibly, the term may derive from *ciuppin*, an alternative name
for the more common *zuppa di pesce* ("fish soup") in some parts of
Liguria. The problem with that theory, however, is that the fishermen who emigrated from Italy to California were not Ligurian but
predominantly from Sicily and Calabria. As Waverley Root put it
in *The Food of Italy*, "As for fish soups, once you dispose of the
special cases, like *zuppa di datteri*, mussel soup, you are faced with
a problem of nomenclature." Even in the special case of *zuppa di
datteri*, you're not on very solid ground: as Root neglected to mention, mussels are known in various parts of Italy as *cozze, mitili,
muscoli, peoci* and *telline* (that last an off-the-wall Tuscan misnomer
for a bivalve in no way related or physically similar to the cocklelike
members of the family *Tellinidae* to which it belongs). *Datteri*,
which are physically and palatally similar to other mussels, are bor-
ers, harvested by breaking apart the soft rocks they drill into. The
word "mussel," incidentally, is from the Latin *músculus*, or "little
mouse," suggested by the mussel's mouselike shape.

There is no unanimity among Louisiana cooks about the proper thickening agent for a good seafood gumbo. Many spiritually espouse the use of filé (powdered sassafras leaves), but at least as many swear by okra. Philologically the okra partisans are on the side of truth and justice: the names of both the green pod and the soup itself are inheritances from Africa, where the Bantu cooked their *gombo* with *nkruma*, the West African progenitor of our own "okra." Sassafras, native to North America, was and remains unknown in the Old World.

A specialty—along with barbecue—of coastal South Carolina, she-crab soup, made with the meat and roe of the "sook," or female blue crab (the male is "jimmy"), needs no further explication. The apparently self-explanatory sources of some other food terms, though, aren't necessarily as conclusive as they seem. Take "barbecue" as a case in point, once dismissed as a case closed in some circles. For generations of French chefs (whose academic schooling traditionally ended at age fourteen), it was taken as an article of faith that the term sprang directly and with no significant alteration from the phrase *de la barbe à la queue* ("from the beard to the tail"), descriptive of a spit-roasted goat skewered from stem to stern. In its sheer plausibility the proposition seemed unassailable. Only problem was that long before the French took a proprietary interest in the term, it had found its way into Spanish, as *barbacoa*, from a noun denoting a wooden frame on which meats were roasted by Taino-speaking Caribbean Amerinds centuries before goats and their beards were known in the Western Hemisphere. (In one of the earliest North American publications of the word used as a verb,

Cotton Mather noted with unseemly glee that a contingent of hostile Narragansett Indians had been "Berbikew'd" in an engagement with New England colonists.)

If anadama bread is still baked and eaten anywhere in the United States, its fanciers are not forthcoming about their preferences. The stuff has been inconspicuously absent from American menus for generations but remains a staple offering of nostalgic cookbook authors and culinary historians simply because of its name. In their writings (as here) the subject is invoked only because of an extremely dubious but persistent folk legend that ascribes the invention of the bread to a conveniently anonymous nineteenth-century fisherman who, supposedly fed up to the ears with his lazy wife's daily offering of cornmeal mush, dumped flour, yeast and molasses into the mixture, muttering "Anna, damn her" while stiring the improvised batter. As with the French barbecue fallacy, the legend is almost certainly an example of spurious hindsight, designed to make sense of a preexistent term of uncertain provenance or meaning. The guess here is that "anadama" is of unknown native American derivation.

A similar story attaches to "hush puppy," the cornmeal fritter still eaten extensively in the American South. It has more credibility going for it than most such folk legends, however, and no really convincing refutation of its presumed origin has turned up. As the theory goes, hush puppies came by their name when scraps of fried dough were tossed to importunate household dogs, with the cook's admonition to "Hush, puppies!" A variant reading ascribes the term to campfire cooks who shared their meals with yapping hunting packs. In the absence of anything more plausible, the inclination here is to accept the story at face value, particularly since hush puppies still are used as emergency dog chow in southern kitchens.

The name of another early American bread, johnnycake, is a corruption of "journey cake" according to some theorists, most of whom credit its origination to black slaves. Made from white cornmeal, salt and water in its simplest form, it certainly could be knocked together during a brief rest stop by wilderness travelers even minimally provisioned for a journey of any distance. Most early eighteenth-century slaves, however, remained in situ once they were settled by their owners, and it seems doubtful that they would have coined a term connoting trips far afield. Moreover, the johnnycake differed in no significant respect from the indigenous basic bread of Mexico and Mayan Central America, the tortilla (as it came to be called after the Spanish conquest, although a tortilla is not a bread but an omelet in Spain). A second, less popular theory holds that "johnnycake" actually originated (as an English noun) as "Shawnee cake" or even "Pawnee cake." The Pawnee can be ruled out; they were plains Indians unknown to English-speaking colonists around the turn of the eighteenth century, when the bread came into fairly widespread use. The hunch in this corner is that "Shawnee cake" has the solidest claim to legitimacy of those advanced thus far. Among many other Amerinds, the Shawnee, an Algonquian-southern tribe, cultivated corn for untold generations before constrained African immigrants were introduced to the New World cereal, and, even had the Shawnee not had a direct acculturative traffic with more southerly pre-Columbians, they might easily and independently have hit on the idea of a thin unleavened corn bread. "Hoecake," incidentally, is generally considered synonymous with "john-nycake" and supposedly takes its name from a cooking technique whereby the blade of a hoe was substituted for a skillet or griddle. Whatever the shape and dimensions of a Colonial hoe blade may have been, a modern gardener would have all kinds of grief trying to use his local hardware store purchase as a cooking implement.

Speaking of hardware, anyone who prepares a ham for baking by studding it with cloves probably experiences a vague sensation of carpentry. The most powerfully and beguilingly scented of the common spices, cloves are the dried immature flower buds of an evergreen, *Syzigium aromaticum*. The earliest recorded references date from the early Han period of China (third century B.C.), when the clove was termed the "chicken tongue spice." The ancient Romans, perhaps more familiar with ordinary carpenters' gear than with chickens' tongues (although they considered most birds' tongues, and peacocks' in particular, delicacies), saw a distinct resemblance between the sharp-pointed flower bud, with its roughly notched "head," and the hand-wrought carpenter's nail then in common use, which was termed *clavus* and successively evolved into the Old French *clou* and our modern English noun. A "clove" of garlic, incidentally, has an altogether different ancestry rooted in the Middle English past participle of "cleave," meaning to split.

The plant known to botanists as *Coriandrum sativum* produces both a spice (its dried seeds) and an herb (its fresh leaves). The herb is commonly termed "Chinese parsley" or "Mexican parsley" in this country, labels that belie its ancient Mediterranean origin but reflect its reintroduction into the American larder via the recent popularity of two alien cuisines. Actually, coriander was one of the first Old World herbs grown in Colonial New England but virtually disappeared from American cookery until just a few years ago. In her 1986 book *Uncommon Fruits and Vegetables*, Elizabeth Schneider asks, "Was there culinary life before cilantro [a.k.a. coriander]? It hardly seems possible that five years ago the fresh herb was difficult to find. . . . Today, with the country's growing Asian and Latin population . . . cilantro is available nationwide." Schneider's use of the Spanish-turned-alternative-English noun reflects the American neglect of the herb between the late seventeenth century and the early 1980s, but coriander was a large part of culinary life in ancient Egypt and among contemporaneous Israelites. In Exodus 16:31 we are told, "And the house of Israel called the name thereof Manna: and it was like coriander seed, white."

To the Chinese, whose recorded use of coriander goes back to Han times, the herb is *hu-sui*, or "fragrant plant," but in English, as in most other modern languages, the common noun derives from a far less flattering perception of the plant's particular fragrance. Our "coriander" is the *coriandrum* of the Romans, borrowed from the earlier Greek *koris*: literally "bedbug," the household pest to whose fetid smell that of the plant's green leaves and unripe berries was odiously—and odorously—likened. While a rose by any other name may smell as sweet, the beauty, or lack thereof, of the Spanish *cilantro*, the Portuguese *coentro*, the Italian *coriandolo* and the Japanese *koendoro* is largely in the nose and on the tongue of the beholder. Ironically, the spice that smelled offensively like bedbugs in ancient Greece is used today to mask offensive odors in pharmaceuticals—usually after it has been fumigated to rid it of insect infestation.

With the emergence of various northern Italian cuisines in this country during the late 1970s and early 1980s, basil, previously unknown to most Americans, became the culinary status symbol of a half-generation. Just as "spaghetti" and "macaroni" had been superseded by the suddenly chic generic term "pasta," we avidly scoffed down our pasta with pesto (so named because its ingredients, basil salient among them, traditionally had been pulverized with a pestle). To the best of my knowledge, pesto made its earliest public appearance on this side of the Atlantic in a restaurant called Fellin's, located on Thompson Street, in Greenwich Village, during the mid-1940s. The *specialità de la casa* was *spaghetti al pesto*, at that time strikingly verdant and fragrant, but the dish wasn't so designated by the management, a family from Genoa, pesto's birthplace. Along with the family surname (Fellini, before the film director invested it with international cachet), the Fellins Anglicized their menu for the benefit of their mostly Wasp collegiate clientele, and *pesto* became "green sauce."

Along with a number of emblematic Southeast Asian dishes, pesto derives its characteristic sprightly fragrance from the herb *Ocimum basilicum*, a member of the mint family that originated in the Old World, probably in India. In both its common and taxonomic nomenclature, the noun is from the Greek adjective *basilikon* ("royal"), in turn derived from the noun *basileus*, or "king." The prevailing theory is that the herb came by its name because it was deemed fit, by virtue of its superb bouquet, only for royalty, but other nouns sprung from the same root include such incompatible concepts as those of the basilica, a Roman Catholic "royal" church of distinctive papal significance, and the basilisk, the legendary dragon from whose supposedly lethal breath and glance the expression "if looks could kill" probably derives. The lizardly basilisk was so termed for its crownlike crest, similar to the plant's flower head, as depicted or described by early monster buffs, who advocated ingestion of the herb as an antidote to the beast's murderous propensities.

Attitudes toward basil have been decidedly ambivalent since ancient times. Revered as *tulsi* in India, the herb was consecrated to the god Vishnu by the Hindus, who traditionally buried a basil leaf with their honored dead. Elsewhere, it often has been reviled as a malignant agent. It was accorded an emphatically mixed reception in Medieval Europe; depending on whom one consulted, it was either mildly benign or flat-out malevolent. Basil was supposed to have been used by Salome to conceal the severed head of John the Baptist and later was put to similar use by Keats in his poem "Isabella, or the Pot of Basil." Precisely why both these decapitators chose to garnish their hidden trophies with what would become the glamor herb of the 1980s remains uncertain. According to Italian folklore, however, there is no uncertainty about the proper cultivation of the herb, whose full, tangily perfumed growth supposedly requires a loud and uninhibited daily cussing out. The superstition probably arose during the Middle Ages, when basil was associated in one way or another with scorpions, which were about as welcome around the house as basilisks. According to one theory, the nasty little arachnids bred under pots of basil. According to another, they bred in the brains of those who inhaled the plant's distinctive pungency. The old Greek root survives in several modern languages: e.g., in the German *Basilienkraut,* the Swedish *basilkört* and the Japanese *bajiru.* I've sonofabitched my kitchen-garden basil year after year, with bumper crops, but have no evidence to indicate that they mightn't have done as well had they been addressed civilly.

Eneas Sweetland Dallas has been little noted nor long remembered since his death in London in 1879. In his day, however, he was a highly respected belletrist (although many of his published writings were unsigned) who, according to the Dictionary of National Biography, precociously applied "notions derived from eclectic psychology to the analysis of aesthetic effects in poetry, rhetoric and the fine arts." Dallas was a respected literary critic of the Victorian era, a friend of John Ruskin, George Eliot, Dickens and the Rossettis, among others, and a first-string obituary writer for the *Times,* where his assignments included the formal obsequies for such deceased eminences as Palmerston, Thackeray and Macauley. He also was the uncredited author of a curious tome published as *Kettner's Book of the Table* in 1877, the ostensible work of a Soho restaurateur, Auguste Kettner, whose establishment still is in operation and renowned for its seasonal game dishes.

Among several other callings, Dallas was a pioneering culinary and gastronomic philologist who, in the volume ascribed to Kettner, sought to set the record straight on a number of cookery terms that had been generally accepted under false or dubious credentials until the publication of his book. He may have been the first reasonably reputable authority to ascribe "John Dory" to the Italian *ianitore*, as noted earlier, although the OED dismisses the ascription, plausible as it may be, as "ingenious trifling."

The same OED is circumspect on the subject of "aspic." Dallas wasn't: "And now, it may be asked, Why is it called *aspic*? There is upon this point the most curious ignorance, although the explanation lies upon the surface." As Dallas went on to say, "Most Englishmen think it must have to do with the asp, and the more readily they remember the question of [Shakespeare's] Cleopatra . . . 'Have I the aspic in my lips?' Even Frenchmen, who ought to have been better informed, make a similar mistake. The great lexicographer, M. Littré, who has produced the standard dictionary of the French language . . . says that aspic is so called because it is cold as a snake. The absurdity of this must be evident if it is remembered that aspic is sometimes served hot; and yet one way or another all dictionaries connect it with the asp."

Dallas goes on to demolish the presumption with irrefutable logic. "It has in truth nothing to do with anything so venomous," he concludes. "It means lavender—in old French, espic or spic; in good old English, spike, lavender-spike, and spikenard. Lavender-spike is to be found in the sauces of Roman cookery." After marshaling a prodigious body of evidence, from Roman cookery onward, in support of his thesis, Dallas concludes that "lavender . . . is not a good seasoning, and it dropped out of account while still the name remained. . . . And so in the course of time it has come about that aspic belongs to a long list of things, which, like houses dispossessed of their first owners, retain names no longer their own—cervelas without brains, orgeate without barley, blanc-manger without fowl, galantine without galingale."

Dallas not only exploded fallacious received wisdom in the realm of culinary nomenclature but mercilessly skewered the chefs of his time who arrogated to their own authorship inconsequential variations on standard recipes and tarted them up with pretentious labels. Eneas, where are you now that we need you, in an age of *salade de bouillabaisse, navarin de fruits de mer* ("mutton ragout of shellfish"), *prosciutto di oca* ("ham of goose"), vinegarless vinaigrettes and various riceless *risotti?*

To anyone interested in the language of food, Dallas's confident assertions and informed speculations are a source of endless delight, and no one of his rigorously analytic bent has graced the culinary literature of this century. His dissection of the term "julienne" goes as follows: "The history of the soup called julienne [the word eventually was extended to include thinly cut vegetables in any form] is lost in the darkness of the past. . . . For a time it was supposed to be named after some cook who invented it; but it was in existence long before the time when any cook was in a position to give his name to any dish; and all the French etymologists have given up the word as a hopeless puzzle." Dallas then embarks on a philological odyssey that carries his speculations from sorrel (thought to have been an essential ingredient of the early julienne formulas) to, more specifically, wood sorrel: "Now this woodsorrel has many names. In France it is known as la petite oseille, l'oseille à trois feuilles, trèfle aigre, surelle, herbe de boeuf, and pain de coucou. In England it is known as woodsorrel, stubwort, sour trefoil, and cuckoo's meat.

But over and above these names there is another, common to both countries and belonging also to Italy and Spain—Alleluia or Allelujah. . . . All persons have not the strong religious sentiment which would lead them to cry Allelujah at the sight of a sour trefoil. In England and also on the Continent the word was corrupted into Lujula. . . . In the south of Italy another corruption was produced: Juliola—little Julia. . . . Is it incredible that the word which in England and some parts of the Continent passed authoritatively into Lujula, and which was transformed in Calabria into Juliola, became fashionable in France as Julienne?"

After further noting that Catherine de Medici, "who first taught the French the refined and scientific cookery of modern times," brought from Italy "Juliola, or some such corruption," Dallas concluded that "the French, with their wonderful habit of Frenchifying foreign names would transform [Juliola] into Julienne."

Well, why not? The French also have naturalized such terms as *rosbif, bifteck* and the plural *pullsover.*

CHAPTER 2

Eating Our Words

The languages in use throughout the world today are as overstuffed as Dagwood sandwiches with food-derived imagery, similes, metaphors and other figures of speech, as were the languages of earliest antiquity. The surviving records of the first civilizations—Babylonian, Assyrian, Egyptian—are in large part grocery lists, and the metaphorical flights of the Old and New Testaments are replete with references to food and eating. Long before the advent of written languages, Neolithic artists depicted the *spécialités de la maison* on cave walls at Altamira, Lascaux and elsewhere: paintings that as far as can be known not only itemized dietary staples but were intended to ensure a dependable supply thereof. Later, in the early age of literacy, Sumerians worshiped the goddess Ninkasi, whose name has been translated by modern scholars as "you who fill my mouth so full." Ceres, the goddess of agriculture (and eponym of "cereal"), was revered much later by the presumably more sophisticated Romans, just as Neolithic peoples had beseeched the beneficence of fertility symbols like the Willendorf "Venus," compared with whose planetary girth figures normally termed "Rubenesque" would be perceived as anorexic.

Let's tune in for a moment to the Song of Solomon: "for thy love is better than wine"; "go thy way forth by the footsteps of thy flock, and feed thy kids"; "My beloved is unto me as a cluster of camphire [i.e., the edible shore green samphire]"; "As the apple tree among the trees of the wood, so is my beloved among the sons"; "I sat down under his shadow with great delight, and his fruit was sweet to my taste"; "comfort me with apples, for I am sick of love"; "thy temples are like a piece of pomegranate within thy locks"; "how much better is thy love . . . than all the spices!"; "Thy lips, O my spouse, drop as the honeycomb"; "honey and milk are under thy tongue." And so it goes, verse after hungry verse, a testimonial to the notion that gourmandise is even better than sex (or, as George Meredith put it about a century ago, "Kissing don't last; cookery do!").

According to Matthew in the New Testament, Jesus demanded of the tempter that he prove his asserted godliness by commanding that stones be made bread, declared that "the blessed are they which do hunger and thirst after righteousness—the salt of the earth" and laced His parables with references to such foodstuffs as grain, mustard seed, herbs, leaven, meal and fish.

Some twenty centuries later, literary conventions haven't much changed. Here's John McPhee, one of the most resourceful stylists now writing in English, falling back repeatedly on food-derived tropes to clarify highly specialized geological terminology for a lay readership: "The beginnings of the San Francisco Skyway, the two-level structure of the Embarcadero Freeway, and [its] many looping ramps and rights of way [are termed] 'the spaghetti bowl' by a leading geologist"; "a big gravelly road cut . . . looked like an ashflow, a mudflow, glacial till, and fresh oatmeal, imperfectly blended"; "In geological ages, just before the uplift, volcanic andesite flows spread themselves over the terrain like butterscotch syrup over ice cream"; "new discoveries of geological events were described as 'popping like corn' "; a jet of water used to flush gold from auriferous gravels "had the diameter of a dinner plate"; the same auriferous gravels "were full of cobbles the size of tomatoes"; early gold-rush affluence soon gave way to "mining for beans"; pyroxene found in the western foothills of the Sierra Nevada was "like a bluewater fish on a farmhouse platter"; "in a subduction zone—a trench between the arc and the continent . . . the continental rock itself reached the trench and jammed it, like a bagel in a toaster."

On a less metaphorical level, what foods do we find in our mouths when we resort to straightforward elements of the vocabulary? When we use the noun "companion," for example, how often does it impinge on our consciousness in its literal sense of "one who eats bread with another?" Similarly, how often do we link the common noun "form" with such cheesy cousins as the Italian *formaggio* and French *fromage*, both from the Greek *formos*, a wicker basket in which certain cheeses were shaped? When we invoke Christ's name are any but the most philologically inclined among us aware of its association with the Greek *chrisma*, or "unguent," the progenitor of our

own "cream"? When we refer to a "union" how readily do we
recognize its kinship to "onion" (except quasi-phonetically), a def-
inite linkage derived from the concept of a whole being something
more than the sum of its parts? When a message is "garbled" (as a
few of the foregoing may be), who among us is aware that the verb
is rooted in the act of sifting grain? And how many of us realize that
a "satire" originally was a dish of mixed fruits, or "compote,"
whence the modern gardener's "compost"? Or that the conceptually
related "lampoon" derives from a French term meaning "Let us
drink"? Or that the mock-Latin verses introduced into satirical literature in the sixteenth century were termed "macaronic" for their
perceived hollowness and compositional resemblance to a dish of
macaroni as it was then known in England? Or that the feather-
capped Yankee Doodle of early American songdom "called him[self]
macaroni" because he was a member, according to the OED, of "an
exquisite class which arose in England about 1760 and consisted of
young men who had travelled and affected the tastes prevalent in
continental society"? (An identifying characteristic of the breed was
its perference for non-Brit victuals, specifically Italian macaroni,
then little known in England, although Ben Jonson specifically had
referred to it in 1599, and the much-earlier first English cookbook,
The Forme of Cury, compiled in the fourteenth century, features
"macrows" as a sort of prototype of today's fettucine Alfredo.)

How many radicals or conservatives realize that their labels derive
respectively from Latin roots that earlier supplied the bases for "radish" and the stewed fruits that our grandmothers termed "con-

serves"? And how many of us are conscious of the saltiness of our language when we bandy about such common terms as "salary," "save," "salvation," "salami," "salivate," "salad," "sage" (the herb, not the wise man) and "sausage" (but not "salacious")—all derived from the Latin *sal* ("salt") and the presumed *salubrious* effects of salt in the diet, recent notions to the contrary notwithstanding?

Our everyday speech is so crammed with more or less unconscious allusions to food and its preparation and consumption that just about anything we have to say in any context will sound like a menu or cookbook recitation. We crab, grouse, beef or carp about what doesn't suit us, quail when faced with a situation we'd rather duck, chicken out altogether under more pressure than we comfortably can handle, and thereby leave ourselves with egg on our faces when we're not reduced to eating crow. There seems to be an inexhaustible supply of food-related figures of speech on tap (beer is a food) for almost any thought or sentiment that comes to mind, and most of them are invoked automatically, with little or no awareness of their boilerplate nature or literal meaning. We don't compare apples and oranges, or so we say of almost any two generically unrelated subjects of discussion. (The orange, incidentally, which ultimately takes its name, insofar as we can know, from the Sanskrit *nāranga*, which survives almost intact in the Spanish *naranja*, was a relative latecomer to the European larder; as recently as the 1630s, the Dutch still-life painter Jan Davidsz. de Heem expatriated himself to Antwerp "because there one could have rare fruits of all kinds [including] oranges." Although the *color* orange is as old as the world, what it may have been called in regions where the fruit was still unknown nobody seems to know. My slipshod research, in any event, has turned up nothing of value.)

We're good eggs or bad eggs, as the case may be, rotten eggs if we hang back at the end of the line while others take whatever plunge may be called for, and we're eggheads if we happen to be intellectually inclined and hit the books before the weather gets so hot that you can fry eggs on the sidewalk while the play you've written lays an egg before its first live audience. Compatible elements in a pairing go together like ham and eggs, metaphorical omelets can't be made without breaking eggs, and Nolan Ryan, in quest of his umpteenth no-hitter, flings goose eggs past opposing batters (without resorting to the beanball or acting like a hot dog). In *Romeo and Juliet* Mercutio tells Benvolio that his "head is as full of quarrels as an egg is full of meat," adding that Benny "wilt quarrel with a man for cracking nuts," while those of us who crave a bit more than we're strictly entitled to are accused of wanting egg in our beer.

We may not know beans, old bean, about this or that, and however much we may apply the old bean (or the Brit loaf) to a given notion, the notion itself may not amount to a hill of beans, although in our enthusiastic endorsement of our view we may be said to be full of beans, if not as full of crap as a Christmas turkey or a plum pudding (the proof of which latter, or any other pudding, is in the eating), or if, indeed, we're not just plain nutty as a fruitcake. Meanwhile, the less imaginative among us merely count beans, whether or not we're string-bean slender or skinny as bean poles.

We may or may not be big butter-and-egg men (or women) in our chosen métiers, but, whether we're in business or show business, we may butter up the big enchilada or top banana if we know which side our bread is buttered on, speaking deferentially, as though butter wouldn't melt in our mouths, while we pour on the sauce, whether it be sauce for the goose or the gander. The verb "to goose"—to poke between the buttocks—has lost its association with a once-common food source with the waning awareness of the behavior of barnyard fowl and animals, and other once-common verbs (e.g., "yean," to bring forth a lamb or kid) effectively have vanished from the living language, useful and evocative as they once may have been.

Despite our modern, urbanized alienation from traditional hands-on food-related intimacies, however, we still don't count our chickens before they're hatched, don't cry over spilt milk and, decades after homogenization, still believe that cream will rise to the top.

We also equate flatness with pancakes and waffle on issues. Those of us who are convinced that half a loaf is better than none put bread on the table and have been termed breadwinners since around the middle of the nineteenth century, roughly a couple of millennia after our remote forebears earned their biblical bread by the sweat of their brows. When not putting bread on the table, we bring home the bacon and have been doing so since the twelfth century, when a side of bacon was awarded by the church in the English town of Dunmow to any married man who could solemnly swear that he hadn't quarreled with his wife for a year and a day. Bacon (from the Old Teutonic *backe,* or dorsal part of the anatomy), like any other meat favored by one man, may be another man's poison, or may have been at least since the middle of the first century B.C., when, according to Lucretius, "What is food to one man may be fierce poison to others" (except, perhaps, among cannibals, for whom one man's meat is another's person).

Of course, we can't have it and eat it both, but what seems to be a piece of cake at the outset of a venture often turns out to be a tough nut to crack: a hot potato that leaves us wondering how we're going to pull our chestnuts out of the fire after biting off more than we can chew.

We invoke all this food imagery so automatically that only the sort of deliberate review of our utterances that few of us ever undertake will demonstrate what a metaphorical hash we tend to cook up in the course of ordinary conversation. Then, despite the facility with which culinary and gastronomic figures of speech may have rolled off our tongues, we may find ourselves eating (a) our words, (b) crow or (c) humble pie. Humble pie? What's the connection between pie (a piece of which most of us want unless it has been launched into the sky) and humility? Well, there wasn't any when the term originated in Britain as "numbles pie," a far-from-lowly dish consisting of beef, veal or venison loin baked in a pastry crust. "Numbles" derived via the Old French from the Latin *lumbules,* a diminutive of *lumbus,* or "loin," whence our own "lumbar" and the aching back our grandparents termed "lumbago."

By the seventeenth century, the loin, a prime cut, largely had been replaced by various innards of venison (castoffs from the dinners of the gentry but nonetheless considered delicacies in some quarters), and "a numble" had given way to "an humble" in the more convenient British pronunciation that has given aitch-droppers "an hotel," "an history," etc. A true humble pie, either in its original orthographic or its later manifestation, would be quite an elegant dish today, a worthy progenitor of one of England's relatively few vaunted culinary specialties, steak-and-kidney pie. Unfortunately, however, the term picked up an undeserved stigma as the language adapted itself to popular usage.

Before leaving the subject of "loins" (girded or not), it may be appropriate at this juncture to explode once more the often-exploded but persistent legend wherein one or another of the royal English Henrys (the gluttonous Henry VIII is usually credited, but various regal namesakes have been nominated), after having demolished a particularly succulent hunk of roast beef, knighted what he'd eaten with the words, "I dub thee Sir Loin." As it happens, "sirloin" is nothing more or less than a corruption of the French *sur longe*, an anatomical descriptive applied to an elongated muscle, and has nothing to do with knights in shining armor.

When we struggle to make ends meet, is one in a thousand of us aware that the ends in question are the corners of the scanty napkins employed by Elizabethan dinner guests at court in their attempts to protect their elaborate ruffs from meat drippings? And trenchant as the beruffed Sir Philip Sidney's, the Earl of Essex's or Good Queen Bess's table conversation may have been, were the principals conscious at the moment of the direct etymological connection between that trenchancy ("trenchant" entered the English language during the first third of the fourteenth century, when it usually was applied to the effectiveness of swords) and their dinner plates, or "trenchers" (which survive marginally today in the noun "trencherman")? Both terms derive from an Old French root having to do with precise cutting, and the original trenchers were simply thick slabs of cut bread interposed between the tablecloth and the viands. The eventual substitution of less porous wooden trenchers in the late Middle Ages may have been regarded at the time as the greatest invention since sliced bread.

Of the individual nicknames adopted by the fifty United States, Connecticut's is the only one concerned with a specific edible. It's also probably the least self-explanatory of the informal state designations. "The Nutmeg State" takes (or, rather, fakes) one of its two sobriquets—the other is "the Constitution State"—from the spicy seed of the hauntingly named *Mystica fragrans,* an evergreen native to the East Indies and cultivated in tropical regions of the Western Hemisphere since the early nineteenth century. It is as ungrowable in southern New England as bananas in Lapland.

Why, then, nutmeg as the icon of Connecticut? Well, the spice was highly priced and dearly prized, as were most others, during the post-Colonial era. At that time, Connecticut had no proprietary claim to it; nutmeg was neither more nor less popular there than elsewhere in the young nation. Such was the value of nutmeg, relative to time and labor, however, that the state's itinerant peddlers— the prototypical shrewd Connecticut Yankees—supposedly mastered a profitable, if somewhat larcenous, trompe l'oeil art form whereby meticulously whittled wooden counterfeits were mixed with, and palmed off on unsuspecting buyers as, genuine nutmegs.

The practice, which would have been deemed ethically reprehensible anywhere else, was proudly flaunted as a prime example of Yankee ingenuity on its home turf, where the scam is commemorated today in Connecticut's nickname.

Other geopolitical entities and many ethnic communities haven't fared as well when food and language have converged to characterize them. In the vast majority of cases, food-derived labels have not been conferred on themselves by their designees but have been applied by one cultural group to another pejoratively, with actual or perceived eating habits or dietary preferences cited as evidence of gross perversity, shared proclivities in many cases notwithstanding.

According to one unverifiable but reasonably plausible theory, for example, the term "Yankee" itself originated as "Jan Kees" ("John Cheese"), an aspersion reserved by Dutch colonists of Nieuw Amsterdam—notable cheese fanciers themselves—for unwelcome later arrivals from England. Major cheese consumers in general have been and remain conspicuously ambivalent about one of their favorite foods: the connoisseur who rhapsodizes over a splodge of *chèvre*, a wedge of Stilton or a smear of Gorgonzola dismissively will term a shoddy garment, an inferior movie or a suspect transaction "cheesy," and the fervent admirer of a well-aged forty-pound round of Parmigiano-Reggiano contemptuously will refer to some self-important functionary or ostentatious big spender as a "big wheel" or "big cheese," terms that go back to the Middle Ages, especially in Holland, but have had less sarcastic connotations in England, particularly among Anglo-Indians, for whom a *chiz*, or a "real chiz," is something like "the real McCoy," "the genuine article." As a common noun for the food itself, "cheese" ultimately derives from the Latin *caseus*, whence also "casein," and survives most recognizably today in the Spanish *queso*. In some of its more metaphorical senses, though, "cheese" probably springs from that same *chiz*, a Persian-Urdu word meaning "thing."

In Great Britain, "hard cheese" is (or was until around the late 1950s) an expression that somewhat ambiguously mingled "hard luck" and "tough shit." During the glory days of movie comedy in Blighty, the gap-toothed actor Terry-Thomas, after maliciously lofting a tropospheric tennis lob into his sun-blinded, cheesed-off opponent's court, would murmur "hard cheese" as cold consolation for his enraged victim. A generation earlier in American gangster films, the perps almost invariably exhorted their partners in crime to "Cheese it!" when the cops arrived on the scene of a felony-in-progress. The best, albeit questionable exegesis of that expression is traced to nineteenth-century England by the OED, which hesitantly puts forth "cheese" as a near-homonym for "cease."

In ancient Greece, according to Reay Tannahill, Anaxandrides contemptuously dismissed barbarian herders as "your butter-eating gentry." To the Romans of the imperial era, gluttonous and sybaritic as their lives may have been for those who could afford their indulgences, the contemporaneous, relatively spartan Etruscan was *obesus*, the big-bellied reveler in "unbridled luxury and indolence." Today, many other Italians term the Tuscans, the progenitors of the Renaissance and exemplars of tasteful restraint, *mangiafagioli*, or "beaneaters," a label with no particular connotations of respect, although beans of one sort or another are eaten with enthusiasm throughout most of the rest of Italy. South of the Rio Grande, Mexicans of the poorer classes are called "beaneaters" by their compatriots, as are Mexican Americans in general by Anglos in South Texas, where the retaliatory slur is *bolillos* ("white bread"). Citizens of Leicester, England, historically have been "beanbellies" in neighboring communities where their dietary preferences aren't shared. Similarly, many Americans continue to refer to the city of Boston as "Beantown," with no particular flattery intended, and Massachusetts in general sticks in some minds as the insular, snobbish "land of the bean and the cod," although the bean supper is a staple of church fund-raisers from coast to coast and codfish cakes traditionally have been a mainstay of blue plate specials nationwide.

One of the abiding mysteries of American English, incidentally, has been the caboosing of "fish" onto a couple of piscatorial nouns that require no more explication than they themselves provide. "Cod" and "tuna" almost invariably are so identified when served as fillets or steaks. Formed into a patty, however, "cod" automatically becomes "codfish," just as tuna from a can becomes "tunafish," especially when it turns up in a salad or sandwich. Obviously, a great many species require the suffix: to find "parrot" or "blow" or "rock" or "cat" on a menu, rather than "parrotfish" or "blowfish" or "rockfish" or "catfish," might lead to some disconcerting conclusions, and the appetency of nobody but circus sword-swallowers would be whetted in the absence of that second, explanatory syllable.

Still, we don't speak of "troutfish" or "salmonfish" or "herringfish."
Why have cod and tuna been equipped with crutches they don't
need?

Speaking of herring (used here in the preferred plural form,
analogous to "trout," "quail" or "deer") and getting back to food-
derived ethnic characterizations, here's William Safire, the celebrated language maven, quoting a "Canadian of British descent" on
the term "Brit": " 'I polled several Brit friends and not one objected
to the word. A more popular word is *kipper* and even the *kippers*
call themselves *kippers*, at least in this neck of the woods. The derivation is obvious.' Obvious to him maybe. It could be from 'English
kipper,' a herring or sea trout cured by smoking and served with
elegance by Mr. Clark, morning headwaiter at Claridge's in London."

Safire cites no source for "English kipper," a term I've never heard
or seen in print outside his column "On Language." To the English
themselves, a kipper (nationality unspecified) was a cured salmon,
a.k.a. "sea trout," long before it became a cured herring. Cured,
convalescent or ailing, the herring never has been termed "sea trout"
in England, but, what the hell, a language maven isn't necessarily a
foodie, and even Homer nodded on occasion, as most of his few
present-day readers still do. In his play *Under Milk Wood,* originally
intended for radio performance, the Welsh poet Dylan Thomas has
his principal character and chorus, Blind Captain Cat, liken a sleeping elderly couple in the fictional town of Llarreggub (palindrome
buffs take note) Hill to "two dry kippers in a box." Whether
Thomas was consciously denigrating juiceless Brits (indeed, whether

he was conscious at all when he wrote the play's final draft, hours before the curtain went up during a monumental binge in New York City) is anyone's guess.

As Safire goes on to note, two other food-based terms are applied by others to denizens of or emigrés from the Scepter'd Isle, neither of them as devoid of slurring implications, or as readily accepted by the Brits themselves, as "Brit": "limey" and, in Australia, "pom." Why "limey" should have evolved into a term of denigration is as unclear as why "kraut," from a vegetable eaten with enthusiasm throughout most of the Western world (and, in slightly variant forms, much of the Orient), became contemptuously associated with Germans alone. In France, where the equivalent but far more hateful disparagement of Teutons is *boche*, or "cabbagehead," *choucroute garni* (the same sauerkraut, embellished with various pork butcher's products) is a perennially popular staple of brasseries and bistros and is occasionally prepared at home for Georges Simenon's redoubtable fictional police detective Jules Maigret, despite Mme Maigret's conviction of its indigestibility. (It was in France, too, that *ma petite chou*, "my little cabbage," became a term of endearment akin to the Anglo-American "honey," "sugar" or "sweetie pie.")

"Limey," of course, is from the limes or their juice provided to English sailors as a scurvy preventative on long sea voyages and, as William Safire puts it somewhat permissively, "is low-class and insulting unless used with jocular affection." Analogously, "penny" would be low-class and insulting if applied to those with sense enough to treat infectious diseases with penicillin. "Pom, from 'pomegranate,' " Safire continues, "is a rough rhyme with 'immigrant,' [a] derogation of immigrants [to Australia] from England."

In some parts—notably the East and West coasts—of the United States a generation or two ago, "corn-fed beauty" was a somewhat backhanded compliment for a pulchritudinous young woman from the American heartland, where swine and cattle were fattened chiefly on corn. And, despite a marked American preference for corn over all other vegetables save the potato, the most important of the native cereal grains historically has been and remains a symbol of condescension, if not outright contempt. The southern socioeconomic put-down for poor or ignorant rustics, "crackers," is a shortened form of "corn crackers," those who subsisted largely on cracked corn, or "grits" (a singular noun in regional usage: "Grits is good"), although the landed gentry were as fond of the stuff as were the less fortunate. More specifically, the term was applied to Georgians by other southerners whose per capita consumption of cracked corn probably was no lower than that of the objects of their contempt.

Throughout the United States, "corny" (supposedly derived from the unsophisticated humor of farmers) is applied to anything smacking of rural naïveté, and a "cornball" remains a yokel whatever his or her (usually his) geographical and cultural origins may have been. Jimmy cracked corn and I don't care.

The verb "to corn" and adjective "corned" (as in "corned beef" and the obsolescent "corned pork" and not much else), incidentally, has nothing to do with American or Indian corn, *Zea mays*, the stuff that grows on tassled cobs, but derives from a generic English term for grains of any sort, including the grains of salt with which meats

are corned and such larger "grains" as peppercorns. The horny nodules that develop on some people's toes are etymologically unrelated
to grains, whether edible or not (as in grains of sand); "corn" in
this sense derives from the Latin *cornū,* or "horn," whose only association with comestibles that comes readily to mind is via "cornucopia," the horn of plenty, symbolic of a superabundance of
edible produce.

Food-related slurs haven't invariably been examples of pots calling
kettles black. The French were and remain "frogs" to English-
speaking outlanders who wouldn't be caught dead eating *cuisses de
grenouilles,* especially the Brits, at least until the Prince of Wales was
conned into trying *cuisses de nymphes aurore* ("legs of the dawn
nymphs") by Auguste Escoffier, the Belle Epoque's *gros bonnet* par
exellence. Early Westerners in Japan were *batu-kusai,* or "butter-
stinkers," to a people who traditionally had shunned the flesh and
fat of quadrupeds. Some Western businesspeople in Japan today
return the compliment by maintaining that the Japanese smell un-
pleasantly of a predominantly seafood diet, although the equivalent
term, "sashimi-stinkers," is used here for perhaps the first time, with
no personal bias intended. The now politically incorrect "Eskimo,"
applied contemptuously to their northern neighbors by other Amerinds, translates as "eater of raw fish" (or "raw meat," depending
on which dictionary you consult), a calumny according to those
who term themselves "Inuit." Before pasta acquired the cachet it
enjoys today, Italian Americans were derided as "spaghetti benders,"
and an airline passenger of Italian extraction remains a "cannoli" in

the argot of flight attendants whose names don't happen to end with vowels. ("Stew," the now generally discredited slang term for a flight attendant, has nothing to do with a simmered dish of mixed foods, but a "steward" or "stewardess" is a ship's or airliner's officer in charge of provisions and their service.)

Back in the days when lard was the cooking fat of choice in the United States, Spanish-speaking newcomers who made use of generally lighter oils were denigrated as "greasers." And despite the perennial popularity of the potato in America, it was the innocent *Solanum tuberosum* that a Californian named Tom Iacino scornfully identified in more recent times with what *The Oxford Dictionary of New Words* defines as "a person who spends leisure time passively (for example, by sitting watching television or videos), eats junk food, and takes little or no exercise." The definition applies to the vast majority of Americans not yet officially pronounced dead. Iacino's coinage was, of course, "couch potato."

At various times, various individuals or cultural groups have been denigrated for what they *don't* eat, and in some cases just for eating. As early as the third century B.C., for example, the Akkadians of Mesopotamia contemptuously termed Amorite herdsmen "a ravaging people . . . who know not grain," and in modern Korea, where beets play no significant role in anyone's diet, a particularly stupid person is a *mujik*, or "beet."

The *mujik*'s American counterpart is said to be "out to lunch," and although the overwhelming majority of Americans eat some sort of midday meal, most of us harbor an amused disdain for "ladies who lunch," the implication, of course, being that ladies who lunch don't do much of anything else, unlike women who work. While the ladies in question are less apt to lunch on slabs of beefsteak or thick chops than on daintier fare, the verb they are tied to originated as a noun denoting a thick piece of food and probably derives from the Spanish *lonja,* or "slice." In the English-speaking world today, the most substantial of the daily three squares is usually the evening meal, which more aptly might be termed "lunch" than "dinner." Until a couple of generations back, though, the midday meal was the big one, especially in rural areas, where nobody lunched but had dinner instead, and "supper" in the evening. Hence, although "lunch" entered the language during the sixteenth century, the word gradually fell into relative disuse until it resurfaced as the term of choice among white-collar types. At the hour when "dinner" was being eaten down on the farm, the "businessman's lunch" was being served in town, at Mom's Cafe. (It was the nonpareil sportswriter Red Smith, incidentally, who cautioned his readers never to play poker with anyone called Doc or eat at a place called Mom's. The latter part of Smith's dictum, which also has been attributed to Nelson Algren, remains one of the two best pieces of restaurant criticism on record. The other? Yogi Berra's "Nobody goes there anymore, it's too crowded.")

Sex and sexism have produced more than their share of food-derived slurs and dubious compliments. For reasons unclear, any reasonably young woman is a "tomato" in vernacular American English, while—less obscurely—uncommonly attractive females have been "cheesecake" at least as long as there have been Hollywood starlets: a possible euphemism for the cruder "eating stuff" or the earlier, even more inelegant "hair pie." The retaliatory "beef-cake" always has had a somewhat tinny ring, probably because the art of cookery has yet to produce such a dish. ("Dish" itself is, of course, a marginally less offensive term for a desirable female, who also may be characterized as "some pumpkins," "a peach," "a honey," "toothsome," "delicious," "delectable" and so on. A virgin is "cherry," a loose woman is a "tart" (or "lemon tart," if she happens to be blond), and a sexpot from below the Rio Grande is a "hot tamale." In the African American patois of the first half of the twentieth century, an attractive woman was "barbecue," and her light-skinned sister of mixed blood (then otherwise termed "high yaller") was a "banana." Today, a vulnerable surrogate female of any race, newly introduced into the penal system, is "fresh fish."

In the Romance languages, the fig (*figue, figo, fico, higo,* etc.) is a metaphor for the vulva, as it has been since Roman times, and a symbol of contempt expressed nonverbally by holding the thumb between the first two fingers of the fist. In French, to make the gesture is to *faire la figue*; the primary occupation of Parisians who moonlight as taxi drivers, it is roughly the equivalent of giving someone the finger in gestural English. Although the pudendal connection, if any, is obscure, a "fig" also is something one couldn't care less about, as in such old expressions as "a fig for" and "[don't] give a fig."

In his book *A Hog on Ice and Other Curious Expressions* (1948), Charles Earle Funk speculated that figs may first have been equated with worthlessness in ancient Greece, where they were a glut on the market. As Funk went on to note, English writers of the sixteenth century termed the obscene gesture "the fig of Spain." The term itself, however, originally was applied to a literal, not merely gestural, fig: one that had been poisoned and, as the OED puts it, "used as a way of destroying an obnoxious person." In any event, "the fig of Spain" was more likely of Italian than Spanish origin. After recapturing Milan in 1162, Frederick Barbarossa is supposed to have avenged himself and his wife for earlier indignities (she had been ignominiously ridden out of town, ass-backwards on a mule) by forcing prisoners to display mule turds between their teeth while pronouncing the words *"Ecco la fica"*: "Behold the fig."

According to an admittedly tenuous theory of my own, to not give a fig may be a bowdlerized variation on to not give a fuck: "To frig" (to copulate or, chiefly in Britain, to masturbate) has been knocking around in the language since Chaucer was a pup, and the second consonant easily could have been mislaid, so to speak, somewhere along the line. "Fig" as a metaphor for worthlessness long since has passed out of living English, but the rhyming "frig" survives as a supposedly sanitized alternative to the precisely synonymous "fuck." In the term's secondary sense, a frigger "beats his meat," "pulls his pudding," "pounds his pork," "chokes his chicken" or is "jerkin' his gherkin."

A pregnant woman has "a bun in the oven" but is more likely to refer to a male's buttocks as "buns" than he is to so designate hers. Gay males (the homophobe's "fruits"), on the other hand, routinely used the expression in references to one another's backsides long before it entered the straight vocabulary, perhaps as a more palatable variation on the British "bum," which latter, the OED speculates, may be a contraction of "bottom." Food-derived similes and descriptives for women's breasts abound in the world's languages and literatures, with melons, pears, lemons, coconuts and bread among those most often invoked. Countless women in the countless novels and *romans policiers* of Georges Simenon, for example, are endowed (or shortchanged, depending on one's view of the matter) with "pear-shaped breasts." During the late 1950s and early 1960s, a leading French produce distributor marketed melons in crates labeled "Lollobrigida" and illustrated with a somewhat hyperbolic rendering of the Italian actress's altogether hyperbolic breasts. In the United States before the replacement of the wooden produce crate and its chromolithographic label by cardboard cartons, around the mid-1950s, nude or scantily clad women were juxtaposed with fruits and vegetables with unmistakable implied interchangeability. Brand names included Buxom, Baby Doll, Nudist and Squeeze Me. Most labels bore depictions of juicy young women in various stages of undress, many of them cupping pears or apples or oranges as though they were breasts, but one portrayed a fully clothed, clean-cut young couple gathering apples in a California orchard. The kneeling young swain's gaze is fixed on his standing inamorata whose skirt is hiking up toward her crotch, ostensibly to facilitate her stretch for a fruit that hangs barely within her reach. The brand name? First Pick.

To particularize further in the same anatomical vicinity, women's nipples, the first source of human alimentation, have been associated metaphorically with nonlactic foods, especially the smaller fruits and berries, throughout history. In the sixteenth-century French painting *Diane de Poitiers in Her Bath*, for example, the king's mistress (apparently still some pumpkins in her fifties) has her nipple tweaked by an attendant, a gesture unmistakably meant to evoke the plucking of a berry or cherry. Conversely, the variety of Spanish cheese called *teta* is so termed for its distinctly breastlike form, nipple included. The Sicilian pastry known as "nipples of the Virgin" was mentioned earlier, and, in another feminine anatomical context, James Jones in *From Here to Eternity* completely bollixed a trope having to do with "a grape plucked and left to wither on the vine."

Male genitalia commonly are referred to as various foodstuffs and vice versa. With no pun intended here, links have been drawn between the penis and sausages from classical antiquity right up to today's American "wiener," the Mexican *salchicha*, etc., and, in the American vernacular, between the penis and pork in general, as in "pork roll," "love pork chop" and just plain "pork." In vulgar English, testicles are "nuts," and the equivalent term in Mexico is *huevos* ("eggs"—*huevos con salchichas*, anyone?). As already mentioned, the avocado was so named by earlier Mexicans for its perceived resemblance to a testicle. In Swahili, *pili-pili* is both an extremely hot capsicum pepper (or the sauce derived therefrom) and slang for "penis." In Louisiana and east Texas, another pungent capsicum is termed "peter pepper" for its distinctly penislike configuration, and the Korean term for similarly shaped peppers, *gohchu*, also denotes the male organ.

If there's a connection between the British "banger" (a sausage) and the verb "to bang" (to have sexual intercourse) I've been unable to find it. According to the OED, a "banger" is also "an astounding lie, 'a thumper.' " Sausages probably were so termed because the integrity of their contents has been suspect since the first pork butcher set up shop. "You will do well," cautions an anonymously written nineteenth-century etiquette book, "not to be talking of dogs when people are eating sausages." As a venerable French chestnut has it, a *charcutier* is haled into court on charges of adulterating his rabbit sausage with horsemeat. After merciless grilling by the judge, he sheepishly concedes that his recipe is "half" *cheval* and "half" *lapin.* Pressed for more specifics, he confesses that the ratio is one horse to one rabbit.

The likening of physical attributes to various comestibles is hardly unique to primary and secondary sexual characteristics. Whether or not we may be having bad hair days, some of us may be "chestnut-haired," "honey blond" or "strawberry blond." Although literal carrot tops are green, redheads remain "carrot tops" until the carotene begins to fade and they become "ginger-haired" while their erstwhile-brunette coevals begin to sport "salt-and-pepper" locks. Our youthful complexions may be "peaches-and-cream," "strawberries-and-cream," "creamy," "milky," "café au lait" or "chocolate," unless we happen to be "olive-skinned," "apple-cheeked" or a "nut-brown maid." In our more choleric moments we may turn "red as a beet" or "red as a lobster," and advanced age may leave any of us "as wrinkled as a prune," spangled with "liver spots" and pendulous with "turkey wattles." If we're small of stature we're "shrimps" or "peanuts," but if we've been plying our "meat hooks" too assiduously we're likely to be "beefy," "porky," "lard-assed" or "beer-bellied." If we border on the anorexic, on the other hand, well, "The nearer the bone, the sweeter the meat."

Despite their heavy reliance on Latinisms for scientific precision, the medical and anatomical vocabularies are as liberally stuffed as the proverbial Christmas turkey with plainspoken edibles. Thus, in English alone we have "milk leg," a painful swelling after childbirth of the femoral blood vessels; "berry aneurism," an abnormal dilation of an artery in the head; "strawberry tongue" and "raspberry tongue," for successive stages of scarlet fever; "strawberry," in the informal parlance of sports medicine, for the bruised thigh incurred by a sliding baserunner; "onion-bulb formation" for layers of tissue growing protectively around exposed nerves; the borrowed-from-the-French *peau d'orange* ("orange peel") for abnormally coarse skin; and the now-obsolete "fig" for piles, which more formally has reverted to the Latin *ficus.*

As the writer Patricia Volk noted while standing in for the vacationing language columnist William Safire several years ago, some of the foregoing and a good many others are in common professional use. Volk went on to itemize "chocolate cysts," "oyster ovaries," "café au lait spots" (sometimes symptomatic of neurofibromatosis, or Elephant Man's disease), "popcorn ball calcifications," "cranberry" and "chicken liver" blood clots, "salmon-patch fammeus" (a benign skin lesion), "apple jelly nodules," "nutmeg liver," "anchovy liver" and "garlic finger," among others, including a cardiac tissue inflammation termed "bread-and-butter pericarditis." Volk omitted pugilism's "cauliflower ear" and stubbed her toe by lumping the lower digital growth "corn" in with food-derived nomenclature, but she bravely bit the bullet (or pullet, if she happened to be dining on chicken) and went on to cite dentistry's "mulberry molar": "a tooth with more than the usual four cusps."

Also on Volk's not-altogether-appetizing menu were "caviar spots" ("little black lumps from the dilation of vessels"), "soupy secretions," "uvula" ("the thing that dangles at the back of your throat," which derives from the Latin for "grape"), "hot potato voice" ("inflammation of the epiglottis") and such anatomical terms as "pisiform bones" (pea-shaped elements of the structure of the wrist) and "fabella," a cranial bone named for the Latin diminutive of "bean." Volk also might have included the generic "vegetable," applied to deeply comatose or brain-dead patients.

Comparisons of the brain-dead and vegetables of no particular variety recently has spawned a whole menu of vegetarian particularizations for the not-overly-bright, who are said to have the intellectual capacities of artichokes, various roots and tubers and other garden produce. The foodstuffs may have changed somewhat, but the equating of mental deficiency with edibles is an old, old story. The butcher's trade earlier supplied us with "meathead," "fathead" and "bonehead"; the greengrocer's with "cabbagehead," "pea-brained," "nuts" and "peanut-size intellect"; the fishmonger's with "chowderhead" and the cook's with "puddinghead." Conversely, our deep thinkers are "eggheads," usually with snide connotations, although dysfunctional brains remain "scrambled."

In its metaphorical uses, ham, the proverbial culinary soulmate of the egg, is a flat-out loser. Despite the widely approved gastronomic symbiosis, a "ham-and-egger" is (or was) a boxer who couldna been a contenduh, a "hamdonnie" or "pork-and-beaner" in the parlance of earlier generations and "dog meat" in more recent times, a frequent diner on "knuckle sandwiches," a bum who eats a lot of leather, a "tomato can." "Ham-handed" or "ham-fisted" is descriptive of klutzy or loutish performances of any kind, and a "ham actor" traditionally has been a "scenery chewer" who "hams it up," usually in "turkeys" that "lay eggs."

The origin of the theatrical phrase "laid an egg" (i.e., failed) is uncertain, but the aforementioned Charles Earle Funk speculated that it may derive from baseball's "goose egg," possibly used for the first time in an 1886 report in the *New York Times*: "The New York players presented the Boston men with nine unpalatable goose eggs in their contest at the Polo Grounds." "Goose egg" (from its resemblance to the figure zero), according to Funk, was a variation on the "duck egg" of British cricket. A show-biz floperoo, by extension, is a production that doesn't score. Or so the theory goes. It might be noted, however, that "laid an egg" is synonymous with "bombed," and that the dropping of bombs from an aircraft (the most nearly avian of vehicles) bears more than a passing resemblance to the act of oviposition. Which came first, the hen fruit or the bomb?

Its dubious contribution to theatrical jargon aside, baseball has added to or borrowed from the American language its share of gastronomic imagery. Although ace moundsmen still pile up those goose eggs by flinging "the old apple" (a.k.a. "onion," "potato") past opposing batters, and triple-A farmhands still come up to the bigs for "a cup of coffee" before reassignment to Podunk, it's been a long while since any major leaguer lugged a "banana stick"—a bat crafted of inferior wood—to the plate, and since the term "can of corn" (an infield pop-up) faded from usage, along with the "crackerjack" (whence the caramelized popcorn brand name) who gloved it. In more recent parlance, however, a snagged fly ball that protrudes visibly above the webbing of a fielder's glove is a "snow cone." The "hot stove leaguer" (a sort of specialized "cracker barrel philosopher") hasn't been heard of much lately, having been superseded by today's vicarious participant, the "rotisserie leaguer," but the "ballpark hot dog" endures in the popular imagination as the epitome of a culinary genre, overwhelming palatal evidence to the contrary notwithstanding. Gastronomic considerations aside, a "hot dog" remains an unnecessarily exhibitionistic player (or, more recently, skier), whether or not he really "cuts the mustard" against pitchers who can really "put the mustard" on their fastballs. Reggie Jackson of candy bar fame, the quintessential hot dog and self-styled "straw that stirs the drink," achieved Cooperstown immortality by belting his fair share of the bases-loaded downtowners that the television commentator and catcher emeritus Tim McCarver terms "grand salamis."

Jackson wasn't a "table setter" (either of the first two hitters in the lineup). As a *batter*, though, he was etymologically related to any thick, beaten culinary mixture denoted by the same common noun: whether a guy who slips a weighted "doughnut" off his Louisville Slugger before stepping up to the plate or a blend of milk, flour and eggs, he or it is descended from the Latin *battuere* ("to beat") via Middle English and Old French.

While we're on the subject, a good many baseball players—seemingly many more per capita than citizens in mufti—have sported names more commonly associated with foods and eating than with ordinary diamond activities. To cite a few examples, we have or have had Clay and Preacher Roe, Dizzy and Steve Trout, Jesse and Ed Whiting, Sid Bream, George Haddock, Thornton Kipper, Bobby Sturgeon and at least four Herrings (Art, Bill, Herb and Lefty), along with John Brill and Roger Salmon (Philadelphia Athletics, 1912, who compiled an unenviable 9.00 earned run average in the two no-decision pitching appearances that constituted his entire major league career). *Esox* (not to be confused with Bosox or Chisox) *lucius* has been personified by Jay, Jesse and Lip Pike. First names attached to Bass include Randy, Kevin, Doc (never heard from again after singling in his sole at-bat in 1918, leaving him with a lifetime average that has been tied but never will be excelled) and the pitchers Dick and Norm (both on the short ends of career records). At least a quartet of Roaches (referring here, in food-related terms, to the fish, not the kitchen pest) have appeared on rosters: John, Mel, Roxy and Skel. And Marlin Henry Stuart exercised his soupbone for three different clubs during his six years in the American League.

To move on from the fishmongers' stalls, baseball menus over the years have featured Pat Duff ("a stiff pudding," from an English variant of "dough"), Walker Cress, Vic Sorrell (so spelled, with a double *l*, around the turn of the seventeenth century), Jack Burdock, George and Wes Curry, Jimmy Mace, Jimmy Lavender, Chuck Laver (an edible seaweed much esteemed in Japan), Hap Collard, Harry Colliflower (a Medieval variant spelling), Ed Bouchee (a savory-filled puff pastry case), Rob Deer, Bob Moose, Ed Roebuck,

Eddie Bacon, Buck Marrow, Harvey Shank and eight guys named Berry, along with Earl Huckleberry, Darryl Strawberry, Bob Lemon and Frank Pears. Also, Joe, Belve and Bill Bean, a sackful of Rices, five little Peppers (not including Pepper Martin or Pierce and Rich Chiles), Zack Wheat, Gene Rye, the delightfully named Herb Hash, three Lambs, Johnny Peacock and Craig Swan. (Although they turn up in few supermarkets today, peacocks and swans were esteemed delicacies from classical antiquity until the late Medieval era.)

Among food-related baseball nicknames we have those of Catfish Hunter, the synonymous Mudcat Grant, "the Georgia Peach" (Ty Cobb) and Peaches Davis and Graham, Ham Iburg, Sweetbreads Bailey, Ribs Rainey, Stew Bowers, a jarful of Cookies (Lavagetto, Rojas, et al.), Pretzels Pezzulo, Shad Barry, Oyster Burns, Bun Troy and innumerable Sugars and Spuds, along with Candy Maldonado, the umpire Beans Reardon, Peanuts Lowrey, a mini-gaggle of Geese (Goslin and Gossage, to name two), Turkey Mike Donlin and Le Grand Orange, as Rusty Staub was extolled during his tenure with the Montreal Expos.

Baseball, it seems, is a hungry game. Other sports yield relatively little of culinary or gastronomic interest: Refrigerator Perry, an up-dated version of baseball's Elton "Icebox" Chamberlain of the 1890s, Pepper Johnson and the Purple People Eaters come to mind in football; Meadowlark Lemon in basketball; Kid Chocolate and a couple of Sugar Rays in boxing; "Champagne" Tony Lema and Andy Bean in golf. Not much else, and nothing to challenge the catcher Johnny Romano, whose nickname, Honey, and surname, a variety of pecorino cheese, combine somewhat incongruously to wind up this meal. Buy me some peanuts and Crackerjack, I don't care if I never get back.

Another of William Safire's pinch hitters, his research associate Jeffrey McQuain (who presides over a syndicated language column of his own), thinks he has spotted a burgeoning food-related trend in American English. "Tasty tropes are sugarcoating the language," he writes. "Not only are *sweeteners* added to financial deals, but *Twinkie defenses* are being used by lawyers who contend that their clients' judgment had been impaired by eating high-sugar food." McQuain also notes that "cookie" is computerese for "an identifying mark . . given to somebody who shares a computer program," while a "*magic cookie* is a pass that allows the computer user to move from one routine or program to another, and *fortune cookie* is a joke or saying shared on computer screens."

Another hacker's term, "menu," was omitted from McQuain's *carte*, but other trendy locutions cited included "flavor-of-the-month" (of which a trendy locution like "flavor-of-the-month" may turn out to be an exemplar if it soon passes out of vogue), "ear candy" for synthesizer music, "electric doughnut" for a strictly telephonic interlocutor, the "lemon tart" mentioned earlier, "do donuts," or joyride in tight circles, and "lollipop psychology," which last puts a sweetened spin on the relatively venerable "pop psychology."

McQuain's thesis, which implies that these "tasty tropes" have given the language a sudden sugar rush, is a bit hard to swallow; the specific coinages he mentions may be recent, but metaphor has had a decided sweet tooth throughout history. "Giving up a steady diet of these metaphors," he concludes, "may not be a piece of cake." It hasn't been since the days of the Old Testament, but that's the way the linguistic cookie crumbles.

Long before the advent of the examples McQuain sets forth as evidence of a recent phenomenon, sugary metaphors proliferated like flies on honey (as opposed to vinegar), and they have stuck in the language since. For generations, it has been as American as apple pie to want a piece of the pie, even though getting it might not be as easy as pie or taking candy from a baby but might, indeed, be as difficult as nailing Jell-O to a tree. McQuain's "ear candy," as he himself notes, has antecedents in the "nose candy" (cocaine) of the mid-1930s and "bubble gum music" of the late 1960s. "Sweetheart deals" stole a long march on today's "sweeteners," and poker players have "sweetened the pot" (i.e., "fed the kitty") since the first straight flush beat a full house. "Saccharine smile" turned up in print for the first time in the 1860s, about three and a half centuries after Leonardo captured one in paint with the Mona Lisa. A pushover in the business world and elsewhere has been a "cream puff" at least since men wore "ice cream suits" in summer and the "sugar daddy" was a staple of Peter Arno cartoons, and an African American suspected of harboring white values has been an "Oreo cookie" almost as long. Especially cushy assignments, appointments and positions have been "plums" since Jack Horner stuck his thumb in a pie, or longer, and any unexpected transactional dividend has been "the icing on the cake" almost since pastry bakers began slathering their productions with crystallized sugar. "Fudge," on the other hand, predates its appearance in the confectioner's lexicon: issues, examinations and contractual commitments were fudged long before anyone devised a recipe for candy by combining sugar, butter and flavorings.

How sweet it is—and always has been.

CHAPTER 3

Unspoken Words,
Uneaten Foods

The symbolic uses of various foods and dining protocols to convey tacit messages goes back to the most rudimentary societies of pre-history. Although there is no documentation to support the idea, it's as sure as God made little green apples that the earliest hunter-gatherers devised crude codes of etiquette that clearly determined who was who in the Neanderthal pecking order. No sooner was the first slain aurochs dragged home to the communal cave than our intrepid spearsman Ugh, whom we met in Chapter 1, doubtless asserted his claim to authority by tearing out the beast's liver or heart, or whatever part he deemed most prestigious, for his own delectation, while his mate, Yurp, the kids and the other kinfolk made do as best they could with whatever he didn't choose as first dibs, probably sucking up to the provider for whatever they got.

Later, more developed societies put more refined spins on the basic concept, but the underlying equation remained the same: prowess determined position, and position determined who ate what. As Margaret Visser notes in *The Rituals of Dinner,* even in cannibalistic societies "there was always the matter of who got which piece, and how much of it." By the early Middle Ages, the remote descendants of Ugh and Yurp—the nobles of the period and their consorts—no longer were knocking their social inferiors upside the head with the femur of the *plat du jour* in order to establish their credentials but instead were seated at the center of the "high table," within easy reach of the salt, then a precious commodity. The lower orders were disposed in seating arrangements at other, literally or figuratively lower tables, "below the salt" in descending importance of rank. Hence, an expression that survives marginally today as a designation for those who don't quite measure up socially.

The noun "treacle," now a benign, chiefly British designation for a kind of sugar syrup or molasses, and in its adjectival form a put-down for oversweet (or saccharine) utterances and sentiments, originally denoted a balm or compound used to prevent or counteract the effects of various poisons, such as the henbane (*Hyoscyamus niger*) of which Hamlet's father got a lethal earful. Poisons played, or are believed to have played, a leading role in the intrigues of Medieval and Renaissance Europe (e.g., the "fig of Spain" mentioned earlier), as did sudden stabbings accomplished while unsuspecting drinkers were knocking back tankards of ale. Two surviving customs commemorate old suspicions. When companionable drinkers light-heartedly clink their glasses together, they roughly replicate the deadly serious ritual of a perhaps more paranoid past: the deliberate intermingling of possibly malign and harmless quaffs as a deterrent to dirty trickery. And when Humphrey Bogart raises a glass and says "Here's looking at you, kid," he's figuratively keeping an eye on a potential assassin through a glass-bottomed tankard enclosed in a silver or pewter sleeve.

The "credenza," the buffet or sideboard on which traditionally hearty English breakfasts are arrayed, also comes down to us from an older device for the circumvention of treacherous foul play. In the Middle Ages, it was known as the "credence table," a piece of dining hall furniture at which implicitly trustworthy courtiers laid their lives on the line by tasting the master's food for poison before it was served to him. (A similar practice survives today among the ethnic Italian peasant families of Yugoslavia's Istrian Peninsula, where it is customary for the eldest female member of a household to sample potentially toxic wild mushrooms before her theoretically-less-expendable juniors risk a bellyache or worse.)

In his introduction to a collection of solicited scholarly essays titled *Food in Chinese Culture* (1977), the book's editor, K. C. Chang, uses the term "food linguistics" to denote the nonverbal communicative functions of food in China. "When a mother cooks the favorite dishes of a home-coming child," he writes, "or a maiden prepares her specialties for a suitor, or a husband makes wined-chicken for his wife who has just given birth, [unspoken] words of affection are being delivered and consumed along with the food. In this regard the Chinese are no different from any other people, but it is the specific words that are used (food variables) that distinctively characterize the Chinese food language."

The vocabulary of that language is enormous, and its inflections virtually unlimited. Ingredients and dishes carry messages not only both individually and in combination with other elements of the meal but in conjunction with the nature of the occasion, the social or economic status of the participants, the number of courses served and their cost, the seating arrangements, the relative simplicity or complexity of the cooking procedures and sometimes the identity of the cook. (An outsider's jump to seemingly obvious conclusions may turn out to be well wide of the mark. In certain circumstances, for example, a quite simple, almost cursory meal may indicate a desire to interact less distractedly with friends or relatives, as may the use of a distinterested cook who allows the hostess to spend more time with seldom-seen guests. Conversely, what an interloper might take to be a lavish tribute to an honored guest might be correctly read by initiates as evidence of the host's low estimate of some visiting schnook's social graces.) All of the foregoing are parts of speech that transmit messages of dead-on explicitness to those who know the lingo.

Throughout their long history, the Chinese have communicated among themselves and with their ancestors and gods, using a specific food language of its own for each group or its subdivisions. Offerings to the dead, for example, may differ markedly, depending on the venue of the ceremony and the relative deadness, so to speak, of the deceased. Indoors, in a hall consecrated to the veneration of the departed, or on a family altar, dead ancestors and other defunct kinfolk retain their living identities vis-à-vis their survivors. As Emily Ahern, one of Chang's contributing essayists, puts it, "They are generally accessible and familiar beings. Consequently, they are offered food that is precisely like the food consumed by those who offer it." At the actual gravesite, on the other hand, one's late grandpa is less a familiar domestic presence, shuffling around the house in worn felt slippers, than a supernatural being who can't just be invited to take pot luck with the family. The death-day offerings of the hall or altar are presented cooked, with an appropriate complement of serving and eating utensils, and are scarfed down by the living when the observance is finished. Gravesite offerings, however, are otherwise untreated dried foods—various mushrooms, fish, bean curd and the like—that without culinary treatment of some sort can't be consumed by living mortals.

At a still further remove, offerings to the gods consist of "the most untransformed food . . . raw fowl with a few tail feathers left unplucked and the entrails hanging about their necks; a live fish . . . and sometimes two stalks of sugarcane, uprooted whole from the ground with roots and leaves still intact." The texts are clear and unequivocal: the "domestic" dead are hardly removed from their survivors and still share their mundane tastes and experiences; the off-premises dead, with at least one foot in the spirit world, are separated from the living by a divide that permits no common experience, even though the elements of such an experience are essentially the same; the gods are altogether estranged from the common practicalities of everyday life and vice versa.

If the Chinese historically have employed foods and the rituals of eating as means of nonverbal communication, their general conversation has been replete with invocations of food and eating as metaphor. On occasions, for example, when most Westerners casually will ask "How are you?" or "How goes it?" the Chinese are more apt to ask (with more genuine concern) "Have you eaten?" In the Beijing dialect, a job is *chiao ku,* "the grains to chew," and a sacked employee says *"ta p'o le fan wan,"* which sounds mournful enough, even to a nonspeaker of the language, and translates roughly as "the rice bowl has been broken."

According to a familiar proverb common to the major wine-consuming regions of Europe, "A meal without wine is like a day without sunshine." The adage seems almost frivolous in comparison with an old Chinese saying that likens a meal without rice to "a beautiful girl with only one eye," but the very concept of a riceless complete meal is a linguistic impossibility in Japan, where the noun *gohan* denotes not only the staple grain but also the meal itself, which is inconceivable without the salient presence of rice. (In other words, you can't sit down to a *gohan* unless *gohan* is on the table.) In the West, *sushi* often is described as "raw fish" or, in a common variant, "raw fish—yuuck," although some versions of *sushi* are fishless and others are garnished with cooked seafoods. To the Japanese, though, *sushi* is rice, and true *sushi* connoisseurs consider its garniture almost incidental to their appreciation of the vinegared grain's infinitely nuanced subtleties. Riceless raw fish is *sashimi,* and, exquisite as it may be in its superior renditions, it doesn't inspire the same sort of reverence accorded *sushi,* the indispensable element of which is the Japanese staff of life. (Similarly, Latin American culi-

nary nomenclature doesn't put the cart before the horse by terming
arroz con pollo "pollo con arroz.") In Japan, as in China and elsewhere in Asia, rice is symbolic of prosperity and good fortune, as it
was in the antebellum American South, where it was known as
"Carolina gold" and actually used as currency. Hence, the rice
thrown at newlyweds is an expression of good wishes for marital
prosperity and, because of its whiteness, a symbol of presumed virginity. In the West, "bread"—the staple earned by the sweat of our
brows, the quotidian provender of the Lord's Prayer—is used less
literally than "rice" is in the East. "*Our* daily bread" may be country
ham with red-eye gravy or bagels and lox or beef and potatoes; to
members of the rice cultures their essential grain may be a metaphor
for any number of other desiderata, but at bottom it remains ineluctably rice.

When Thomas E. Dewey ran for the American presidency against
Harry S. Truman in 1948, the Republican challenger was characterized by some detractors as "the little man on the wedding cake."
With his meticulously groomed moustache, dark tailored suits and
immaculate haberdashery, Dewey doubtless lost a few votes in a
squeakingly close election when perceived as a mere pastry decoration. His opponent, the ultimately victorious incumbent—an em-
barrassingly premature Chicago newspaper headline to the contrary
notwithstanding—generally was accepted as a "piss-and-vinegar"
personality, the diametrical opposite of today's "vanilla" wimp or
"cookie-cutter" conformist.

While the nuptial couple are depicted in minature on many wedding cakes (lying together in the marriage bed rather than standing at the altar, in some Hispanic American renditions), it's Margaret Visser's eminently plausible contention that "the cake [itself, regardless of its representational embellishments] stands tall, white, archaic, and decorated, pyramidal like the veiled bride herself, and dominating the proceedings; it is a version of the bride, and the piercing of it [the cutting of the cake and, usually, the sharing of the first slice between bride and groom] dramatizes her rite of passage." The symbolic implications of the ceremony, of course, presuppose bridal virginity, a more-often-than-not unfounded supposition these days.

In some parts of Italy, the eligibility of prospective brides traditionally has been judged by the quality of their renditions of regional specialties. In Abruzzi, for example, a nubile young woman advertised her desirability by serving a superior version of *maccheroni alla chitarra* or "guitar macaroni," so called for the wire-strung frame on which sheets of the pasta dough were cut into strips. The French, more inclined to wait for sustained postmarital evidence of culinary skills, apply the term *bonne femme* ("good wife") to the sort of dishes that a hungry husband looks forward to after a tough day at the office: a term that may be rendered obsolescent by the advance of political correctness. In many of the same communities, especially around Venice, a suitor serenades his prospective bride by crooning these lyrics: "I like *bigoli* [a sumptuous handmade version of spaghetti], Maria [or whomever], with *luganega* [a type of sausage] . . . Maria, serve it please."

In Japan, clam soup traditionally is served at Shinto wedding feasts, the paired valves of the mollusk's shell symbolizing the bridal couple's union, and in Sung Dynasty China the family of the groom was presented with a gift of steamed pastries called "honey-harmonizing-with-oil cakes" as a metaphor for the presumably felicitous new familial relationship. For reasons less evident, small, separate dishes of salt and lemon are served to the bride and groom at a Polish wedding reception, as an expression of good wishes for the couple's future health. Every culture communicates its nuptial expressions of good will in similar food-derived symbols, the origins of most of which have been lost with the multiplication of generations. To itemize them all would fill more volumes than I've contracted to write.

From the Neolithic epoch onward, various foods have played prominent iconographic roles in the visual arts, conveying wordless messages of faith, hope, despair and social commentary. The earliest cave paintings and bone engravings were concerned exclusively with food and its procurement by hunters and fishermen who advertised (or perhaps solicited) their prowess in depictions of what they ate or hoped to eat. Significantly, the Neolithic artists of Western Europe were childishly primitive self-portraitists who represented men as little more than disproportionately small stick figures but delineated their prey with striking verisimilitude. Relatively small game, such as a goat in a Spanish cave mural, might be blown up three times its actual size in scale to the hunters who surrounded it, but the beast and its movements were observed with a degree of fidelity that painters remained incapable of applying to the human figure for another ten thousand years or so.

It would be a gross overstatement to maintain that all food in art has symbolic or allegorical messages to convey. Just as Freud's famous cigar was sometimes neither more nor less than a cigar, Cézanne's apples and Chardin's breads were neither more nor less than apples and breads: convenient props (they didn't fidget, as Mme Cézanne might have, halfway through a tiresome sitting) for painters concerned strictly with painterly problems. The subjects of Vincent Van Gogh's *The Potato Eaters,* on the other hand, or Jean Millet's and Camille Pissarro's impoverished potato gleaners, or Picasso's sharers of *The Frugal Repast,* are the stuff of social commentary that goes beyond purely formal considerations.

Similarly, the foods, culinary procedures and eating rituals depicted in the paintings and relief sculptures of pharaonic Egypt and Greek pottery decoration were vehicles for the documentation of how life was lived in its time and at its most elemental level. Later art, however, increasingly made symbolic and metaphoric use of food motifs. The pomegranate, for example, practically bursting with seeds, was symbolic of fertility in Medieval art and figured prominently in many portraits of the Virgin and Child; the apple, of course, was emblematic of original sin. Later, during the seventeenth century, Dutch still-life painters such as Jan Davidsz. de Heem provided their contemporaries with cautionary mementi mori (reminders that all things, including life, pass) in the form of lavish tablescapes crammed with meticulously rendered spreads of boiled lobsters, deteriorating lemons, overripe grapes, broken pomegranates and tumbled crockery and tankards. So central was food to de Heem's "message" that he eventually left Holland for Antwerp, where, as Reay Tannahill quotes him in her book *Food in History,* "one could have rare fruits of all kinds, large plums, peaches, cherries, oranges, lemons, grapes and others, in finer condition and state of ripeness to draw from life."

It was the Italian mannerist Giuseppe Arcimboldo, though, who made a visible language, or at least an alphabet, of nothing but comestibles. In his singular caricatures, such as his lampooning portrait of John Calvin—depicted as neither fish, flesh nor fowl but an unappetizing hodgepodge of all three—the ambivalent subject can be read alternatively as a human figure in profile or the contents of a well-stocked larder. Stealing a march of sorts on the eighteenth-century French gastronome Brillat-Savarin ("Tell me what you eat, and I will tell you what you are"), Arcimboldo says, in so many image-words employed as double-barreled nouns that simultaneously denote both specific foods and specific anatomical features, "I'll show you what you eat and show you what you are."

In his less personally targeted paintings, such as his allegorical *Summer* of 1577—a health food nut's *menu de dégustation* of vegetarian offerings, with assorted edibles at once representing themselves, their ostensible subject and even articles of clothing—Arcimboldo constructs a figure in profile, its features made up entirely of fruits, berries, vegetables and grains. He makes a figurative cliché like "cherry-red lips" literal by representing lips as cherries (or cherries as lips), punningly substitutes an ear of corn for the anatomical ear denoted by the Italian noun *orecchio,* somehow manages to anticipate Gertrude Stein's best-known line by some two and a half centuries, as he informs the viewer that a nose is a nose is a zucchini, and generally plays hob with the conventions of visual communication and perception. If the chemistry of the paint itself is taken into account, the question becomes "Animal, vegetable or mineral?" Seen from a distance, the personification of summer is a reasonably plausible likeness of a grinning man, perhaps even the artist himself, whose name is spelled out in full, in trompe l'oeil block letters, across the collar of a tunic woven of wheat straws, not far from the dead center of the canvas and looking much more like an identification badge than a signature. Up close, the painting is a completely plausible, if somewhat contrived, arrangement of high-summer produce. Giuseppe, you sly dog, you really painted a mouthful.

> *In short, food is communication. No conclusive or important business can be transacted, no firm contacts made, no importance marked or asserted, without the sharing of food. The expense, status value, quality, and setting of the food communicated more about the critical social dynamics of the situation than language can; much that is hard to verbalize, and more that would be impolite to verbalize, is communicated by this channel. Such use of food is worldwide, as every anthropologist knows; but no culture has developed it more than the Chinese.*
>
> —E. N. Anderson Jr. and Marja L. Anderson in
> *Food in Chinese Culture*

The communicative functions of food in China *are* more highly developed than anywhere else in the world. In the modern West, the sharing of meals is accepted as generally expressive of familial love and solidarity, interactive sociability, esteem, respect, commiseration and the like, with further particulars left relatively undefined. It also can be a not-so-thinly-veiled assertion of control, or even contempt, as demonstrated by the aggressive restaurant check-grabber or the interminable blather of the wine snob.

In Western Europe, and even more so in the English-speaking former British colonies, all these messages, manifest as their content may be in broad outline, don't much tell it as it is in any detail. Except on a dwindling number of ritual occasions (e.g., La Vigilia, the traditional Italian meal eaten on Christmas Eve and made up of seven meatless courses in some households, nine in others, respectively symbolic of the seven sacraments and the Holy Trinity tripled), many of which themselves have lost much of their symbolic meaning, the composition of the menu is either arbitrary or dictated by rote response to ill-defined traditions, and the content and preparation of individual dishes are determined by purely aesthetic concerns and accepted notions of culinary compatibility. (As just about everyone—including the food and beverage manager of a Taipei hotel—knows, for example, lox "goes with" cream cheese, not with peanut butter, and a stack of flapjacks calls for maple syrup, not béarnaise sauce.) Ingredients, whether individually or in combination with others, haven't much to say for themselves; they lie mute on the plate, imparting no information concerned with anything but their intrinsic properties, their contrast to, or harmonization with, their bedfellows and the proficiency of the cook.

In marked contrast, any meal in China crackles like a shortwave radio with all manner of coded messages, many of them overlapping and most infinitely nuanced. From the seating arrangements and number and quality of courses to the last bowl of rice (served at the meal's end but left untouched, to signify complete satisfaction with what the host already has provided), each element of the assorted offerings, including textures, colors and the five canonical flavors (sweet, sour, briny, bitter, pungent) has its shades of meaning, whether singly or in combination with others, depending on the nature of the occasion or the relative stature of the various participants. We're not just talking fortune cookie messages here: Supposedly transferable attributes of just about every dish or ingredient (e.g., longevity conferred by braised turtle; the good fortune, auspicious occurrences and religious piety signified by red and orange fruits in combination), whether transmitted between fellow diners, diners and deceased forebears or mortals and gods, traditionally have been apparent at a glance or bite, and their significance has been understood from the moment the grub hit the table. Because the tables usually were round, the position of honor was situated at the north, facing the entrance to the house or room, with the second most prestigious placement opposite. During a tour of China in the early 1980s, I found myself facing the seventy-eight-year-old vice president of Chungking University across a banquet table. He occupied the place of primacy by virtue of his rank, chronological seniority and reputation as a world-class boozer. An alumnus of

Purdue, Professor King spoke excellent English and was well informed on Big Ten basketball circa 1935. I knew nothing of Big Ten basketball circa 1935 (or circa anytime else) but had been touted by an advance man as the professor's round-eyed, elbow-bending counterpart and therefore occupied a position for which I had no other credentials.

To my dismay, I was informed that the professor and I were to duke it out, drink for drink and *mano a mano,* the weapon of choice (his choice, not mine) being *maotai,* which bears no resemblance to the somewhat cognate *mai tai,* a tarted-up cocktail usually garnished with a miniature paper parasol and served to egregious rubes in Sino-Polynesian restaurants. The real McCoy is roughly comparable to the most corrosive versions of home-distilled French *marc* or Italian *grappa* but packs a kick that would knock the breath out of any French or Italian lush. I managed somehow to drink the old Indiana basketball buff under his primary position at the table but couldn't get the vile taste of the schnapps out of my mouth for a week.

It was at the same table that I committed the unpardonable gaffe of talking about matters that my hosts tacitly had spelled out in a language I simply didn't comprehend: the ritual language of the food set before us and all its appurtenant ceremonial. As older and wiser China hands before me had discovered to their chagrin, you can't discuss anything of import at a Chinese banquet because all the talking is done by the food.

In the rice-growing provinces of southern China, where the staple has been cultivated by stoop labor for thousands of years, each individual grain has been equated with a drop of human sweat since time immemorial. For reasons unclear, since the apricot traditionally has been an auspicious symbol for the Chinese, syphilis long ago was termed "the apricot disease" and generally was deemed curable only "when the bamboo fruits" (i.e., bears fruit), which is to say, almost never. In southeastern China (and more specifically in Hong Kong today), ginger is symbolic of fertility, and the term for lotus seeds, *lien tau,* has a close, somewhat punning cognate in a wishful phrase meaning "many sons." Anywhere in China, to neglect to raise a bowl of food almost to one's lips is to insult the host by indicating a lack of interest in what has been offered.

Bemused Westerners, confronted in Chinese restaurants by such menu terminology as "dragon and phoenix," "lovers in the stars," "lion's head," "hundred-year-old eggs" and the like, are inclined to dismiss the nomenclature as entrepreneurial flights of fancy, originally composed to titillate appetites that might not have been as readily aroused by more straightforward descriptions or itemizations of ingredients. In almost all cases, however, they are literal translations of old terms laden with religious, mythic or folkloric meaning.

No egg, of course, would be edible a century—or even a few months—after it was laid, an uncommonly effective preservation technique notwithstanding. But according to conventional Chinese wisdom, the regular consumption of eggs promotes longevity. Hence, the preserved food symbolizes its eater's presumably rosy actuarial prospects, making a slight blurring of the lines between the aliment's putative age and the eventual shelf life of its ingester understandable enough. (A couple of years ago, a dozen sooty duck ova, purchased in a grocery in New York's Chinatown, noisomely deliquesced in their shells after a few months of fetching display in a basket on a kitchen counter. The damned eggs had to be discarded instantly when the first of them was cracked open. Last time I looked, I was still around to tell the tale.)

During a tour of southern China some years ago, I was introduced to a gnarled little peasant woman who seemed remarkably feisty for a locally reputed ninety-eight-year-old. Pressed for the secret of her staying power in a region where people are eighty before they're thirty-five, she replied that she'd eaten an egg every morning of her life since she'd been weaned.

At first blush, irony, rather than literalism, also seems to play a part in the naming of some Chinese dishes. To take one example, "beggar's chicken" is a rather sumptuous production, nomenclaturally comparable to such facetious Western constructions as "beggar's purse" and "beggars on horseback": offerings that seem relatively modest at first glance but turn out to be outrageously epicurean on further investigation. The Chinese label supposedly is anecdotal and derives from an old folk legend about an actual beggar who stole a chicken, wrapped it in mud and buried it in the ground, beneath a fire, to hide it from military marauders who otherwise would have requisitioned the bird and done away with the cook. These days, a stiff dough usually is substituted for the legendary clay; after a mallet and chisel have been plied on the rocklike exterior, an infinitely fragrant, flavorsome and tender finished product is served forth, crammed with all manner of rarefied goodies. Conversely, the grass-hopper, eaten by the poor in some parts of China, is termed "brush-wood shrimp," and a rather nondescript vegetable ragout favored by a toothless dowager empress of the Ching dynasty was glorified by a name that translates loosely as "brocadelike."

The Chinese also frequently have named individual ingredients for their perceived effects on their consumers. As a case in point, the mildly soporific root of the marsh trefoil (a.k.a. bogroot), whose leaves E. S. Dallas identified as the definitive component of "the soup called julienne," traditionally has been known as *shiu ts'ai,* or "sleep vegetable," in China.

Whether tacitly expressed, nomenclaturally overt, euphemistic, or gently ironic, the messages carried by foods, their names and their formalized consumption in China constitute an infinitely nu-anced sublanguage that has no equivalent in the West. As Lin Yu-tang put it in *My Country and My People,* "If there is anything we are serious about, it is neither religion nor learning, but food." The only problem is, you're hungry all over again half an hour after you get up from the table.

CHAPTER 4

Say What?

In retrospect, it seems almost inevitable that the verb "to garble" would be concerned with food—specifically, as noted earlier, with the threshing of grain. From just about Day One, when some primeval hunter-gatherer emitted an appreciative grunt, in lieu of a formulated part of speech, for whatever he was stuffing into his face, much of the world's food nomenclature and terminology has been the upshot of garbled transmission or reception, of mistranslations, misattributions, bollixed notions of provenance or growth characteristics, confusion of every sort. Coincidentally, "gobble" is an etymologically unrelated near-homonym of "garble," and the "gobbler" derived therefrom is, onomatopoeically, a turkey: either the North American bird *Meleagris gallopavo* or the related *Agriocharis ocellato* of Mexico and Central America. As it happens, the common noun applied to both is a misnomer: not only a misnomer, but a misnomer *derived* from a misnomer.

The first "turkey" to bear the name was a pheasantlike Old World

bird of the family Numididae, *Numida meleagris,* native to the West
Coast of Africa and, more specifically, Guinea, once part of the
Roman province of Numidia. Known more properly as the guinea
fowl or guinea hen today, it found its way to the kitchens and tables
of Western Europe during the fifteenth century from Turkey, via
the island of Chios, off the Turkish coast, where Genoese trading
ships, notably those under the command of Christopher Columbus,
had established mutually beneficial commerce with the Turks.

The identity of its region of origin having blurred somewhat in
transit, the fowl arrived in Europe bearing either the label "turkie
bird" or "guinea," probably depending on the knowledgeability of
the individual shipper. A predecessor of, say, Frank Perdue might
have favored one designation, while a competitor might have chosen
the alternative in order to distinguish *his* oven-stuffer from proto-
Perdue's. (Later, Shakespeare would hedge *his* bets by using the
terms interchangeably: what was "turkie" in *Henry IV, Part I* subsequently became "gynney hen" in *Othello.*

Either Columbus himself, always quick to stick a conveniently
ready-made label onto anything already known or anticipated in a
more or less similar form (e.g., "yam" for the sweet potato or "Indian" for Carib), or some similarly inclined early arrival in North
America, saw a bird that bore a passing resemblance to one he'd
either eaten or couldn't afford to eat in the Old Country, put two
and two together, came up with a bottom line of six (not including
tips and taxes)—and now we're all stuck after Thanksgiving with
doubly misnamed leftovers.

Language muddles along, making do however it can with imprecision, crutching from unsure step to step on its "you-knows." (*You*
know what I mean, even if *I* haven't formulated the thought clearly
enough to articulate it, y'know?) As a tadpole, I "dove" into the ole
swimmin' hole in the Pocono Mountains of Pennsylvania, with the
approval of my grade school English teacher, but the last Olympic
contestants "dived" into their pools. Acts of God—hurricanes,
earthquakes, tornados and the like—"wrought" havoc when I was
a kid but recently have "wreaked" havoc in the *New York Times.*
(Is that fence outside the park now "wreaked iron"?) The *Times,*
too, has told us that "a stand-up guy," New York governor Mario
Cuomo, "*lays* down [emphasis added] for a good cause" (blood
donation). At least one former president and a recent secretary of
defense pronounced the *N*-word *nucular,* the shortest month becomes *Febyouary* in the mouths of radio and TV announcers, and
every rule that once governed the use of pronouns routinely is
flouted by the shapers of our speech. "Exotic," the favorite adjective
of food writers these days, is applied ad nauseam to native ingredients, many of which now come to the table "deboned," and a
nationally circulated resort advertisement invites prospective vacationers to "languish" beside a heated swimming pool.

Tempting as it may be to ascribe the debasement of language to
such malign recent developments as the ascendency of electronic
communications over the written word, the sound bite over sub-
stantive information and a general sloughing off of educational rigor
in favor of lowest-common-denominator permissiveness, the fact is

that the oldest of languages, the language of food, has lacked precision from the get-go and has been marked by sloppiness since the first primal grunt.

Much of the confusion in food terminology arose at times when a great many foods truly *were* exotic: when they were newly imported edibles for which no terms existed in the languages of the importers. Exploration, commerce and conquest in the ancient world produced a panoply of previously unknown foodstuffs. Medieval Europe underwent a similar experience when the Crusaders brought unimagined comestibles home from the Near East, along with variously mangled versions of their Arabic names. Later, the discovery of the Americas revolutionized eating in the Old World with a bewildering array of new foods for which the only existing names belonged to languages altogether unconnected to Indo-European roots and therefore particularly susceptible to misconstruction in an age when linguistics were notably inexact and standardized orthography was nonexistent.

Throw in relatively undeveloped powers of observation and analysis of the unfamiliar (even as keen an eye as Albrecht Dürer's was unable to see unfamiliar beasts without an overlay of myth; compare his supremely confident, minutely observed *Hare*—an everyday market animal that all but quivers on the page—with his clunky, anatomically unworkable, crocodile-hided *Rhinoceros*). Then stir in a heavy dose of the sort of superstition that gave the language "barnacle goose" and a natural tendency to define the unknown in terms of the known, and nomenclatural confusion is bound to follow.

Prudery, too, has been known to affect food terminology. "Dandelion," for example, is from the French *dent de lion* ("lion's tooth"), a name given to the salad green around 1740, for its dentiform leaves. Until then, however, the generally accepted term had been *pissenlit* ("piss in bed") in France and "pissabed" in England, for the green's diuretic effect. Eventually, the French reverted to the pissier noun, but the English-speaking world retained the prissier alternative. The raunchier word was used metaphorically by Victor Hugo, for whom the dead "*manger des pissenlits par la racine*: "eat dandelions by the root." Well, it beats pushing up daisies when you're hungry.

Although *dent de lion* remains more or less recognizable in its English transmogrification, especially when spoken, other French terms have been mangled to the point where identification of their origins is all but impossible in a language that has managed to make "kickshaw" of *quelque chose*. Even when the original pronunciation remains roughly intact, altered spelling often obliterates clues to a transplanted term's derivation. As a case in point, "demijohn" would seem to be a real stumper at first blush. The natural assumption would be that the prefix "demi" signifies "half" or having less than full status (e.g., "demigod," "demimonde," etc.), but bottles with capacities of up to fifteen gallons aren't precisely half-pints and hardly would seem to be mere 50 percent solutions to the problems of bulk shippers of wine, spirits or vinegar. Moreover, who was John in *this* avatar? The same guy who gave his name to John Dory, hoppin John, St. John's bread and, more casually, to johnnycake, jack mackerel, amberjack, Crackerjack, flapjack, jackfruit, applejack, et al.? Is half a john a *jo*, a *hn* or a two-hole privy with one hole out of commission?

The word's early ancestry is uncertain; undocumented speculation has ascribed it to possible Arabic and Persian roots, and it turned up in various forms on the Continent before its adoption into English. What *is* known with relative certainty is that it entered English around the turn of the eighteenth century via the French term *Dame Jeanne* ("Lady Jane"). The identity—indeed, the nationality—of the lady in question isn't known. Perhaps she was Lady Jane Grey, who wore the English crown for ten days and nights before it was removed in 1553, as was her head the following year. The bottle, usually robed in wickerwork, is full-bodied beneath a long slender neck. As is the case with most bottles, it has no head.

Whereas most demijohns were used as shipping containers from Continental Europe to the New World (principally the West Indies) during the late sixteenth and early seventeenth centuries, some doubtless turned up in England, in lieu of barrels or individual bottles, as conveyances for various wines, mostly fortified, to which upper-class Brits rapidly were becoming addicted. The English genius for reducing alien proper nouns to simplifications that would roll trippingly off the tongue soon converted the place names of various Continental entrepôts to generic terms that could be pronounced with relative facility from beneath a stiff upper lip. Thus, the fortified wines of Xeres de la Frontera, in southwestern Spain (where the *frontera*, or "frontier," had been repositioned often, as Spanish territory encroached on Portugal's) became "sherry"; the wines of Oporto, in Portugal, became "port"; the German *Hoch-heimer Wien,* a white from the Rhine Valley, became "hock"; and a sweet fortified wine originally produced in Greece under the name of Monembasia, the port from which it was shipped (the Medieval Latin place name was Malmasia) became "malmsey," which survives, albeit tenuously, today. "Claret," the English term for Bordeaux wines collectively, entered the language by way of the Old French from the Medieval Latin (*vinum*) clārātum, or "clarified wine."

The garbling of food nomenclature hardly is restricted to Anglicizations of foreign terms. I'd been baffled for years, as I'd been by *melanzane alla parmigiana* (see "Hors d'Oeuvre") by the name of a sumptuous regional Italian treatment of baked lasagna, a specialty of the Marches listed on a few Italian-American menus as *vincisgrassi.* Consultation of various dictionaries, cookbooks and food histories shed no light on the subject, and the few American restaurateurs who featured the dish had nothing to offer in response to my inquiries. Was *vincis* a spinoff of some sort of the Latin *vincere* ("to conquer," as in Julius Caesar's *"veni, vidi, vinci,"*) or had it anything to do with Leonardo da Vinci's hometown? *Grasso,* I knew, meant "fat" (Bologna, a city renowned for what may be the best eating in Italy, is known as "Bologna la Grassa"); hence, *grassi* presumably would be "fats" in plural form. Still, no stretches of the imagination came anywhere close to resolving the question. Then, somewhat belatedly, I happened on a copy of Waverley Root's *The Food of Italy,* published in 1971. Here is Root on the subject of *vincisgrassi*:

Ascoli Piceno, the Asculum of the Romans and the capital
of Picenum before the Romans arrived, is also the capital
of the inland cuisine, and very much aware of that fact.
It must stick in the craw of Ascoli gastronomes to realize
that the paternity of one of the most notable dishes of The
Marches belongs not to Ascoli but to Macerata. This is
vincisgrassi *(in local dialect* vincesglasse*), a name so un-*
usual and so impenetrable that many gastronomic writers
have abandoned the attempt to unravel its meaning, and
no wonder, for its source is somewhat curious. The dish
was invented in 1799 by a chef of Macerata in honor of
the commander of the Austrian forces based at Ancona,
and was named for him. Vincisgrassi *immortalizes, not*
too efficiently, Prince Alfred zu Windischgrätz.

Case closed.

As Root also pointed out while still occupied with the same region, the Marches, a specialty of Pesaro, the birthplace of the com-
poser Rossini, is a dish called *tornedò alla Rossini* ("a round cut of
steak cooked in a casserole with ham, mushrooms, parsley, pepper
and lemon"). As Root also was quick to note, "This is a far cry from
the *tournedos Rossini* known all over the world, which is grilled and
is distinguished by a slice of foie gras balanced on top of the steak.
Tournedos Rossini is a French creation, named for the musician who
was the idol of Paris, where he lived for many years and where he
died. It is possible that Pesaro was spurred by the example of Paris
to produce itself a dish to honor its most famous citizen." *Tournedos*

(or *tornadò*), incidentally, is sliced tenderloin of beef, so called because the butchers' stalls in the now-defunct Paris market Les Halles
turned their backs (*tournant le dos*) on the fresh fish department.

Mention was made a few paragraphs back of Bologna, the capital
of Emilia-Romana and the generally acknowledged gastronomic
capital of Italy. The city's name has been dubiously honored in
American English as "baloney," of which hot air purveyors have
been full for generations. Although the sausage so termed is more
formally labeled "bologna" by its American producers, the accepted
pronunciation remains *baloney*, and in some written contexts the
"proper" term would seem a glaring affectation. (When a reference
to a "baloney sandwich" was "corrected" by the copy editor of a
Goody Two-Shoes food magazine I used to write for, the tenor and
meaning of the whole sentence went kerflooie.) As it happens, neither form of the common noun is known in Italy, where the emblematic sausage of Bologna, from which the American deli cold
cut ("a pale reflection of Bologna's own special sausage" in Waverley's Root's words) derives, is called *mortadella.*

The etymology of *mortadella* is debatable. According to one theory, the term comes down from Roman times, when a particular
type of sausage was called *murtata* for the myrtle berries with which
it was flavored (*mortella*, "myrtle" in modern Italian, is a favored
flavoring agent in Sardinia, where it is used, to the bafflement of
outlanders, as the salient ingredient of a popular form of *granita,*
the pebble-textured water ice so termed for its resemblance to
crushed granite). Trouble is that the sausage has been flavored not
with myrtle but with peppercorns, at least since the fifteenth cen-

tury, when peppercorns were the luxurious equivalent of today's caviar, truffles and saffron and, indeed, were used as money. A far more likely explanation of the origin of the word goes back to the last quarter of the fourteenth century, when the monks of Bologna were the city's *salumiere* (pork butchers) and the Corporazione dei Salaroli (Guild of Sausage Makers) was founded. (Both "sal" words, along with "sausage" itself, derive from the Latin for "salt.") The good friars produced the fine textural uniformity of their product by laboriously pounding the ingredients in a mortar, with a pestle. (The pestle, as already mentioned, gave pesto its name, although that name may be changed to "processo" now that most pestos are whipped up in jig time by increasingly ubiquitous electrically driven kitchen appliances.) Hence, the thinking goes, *mortadella* may be a truncation of *mortaio della carne di maiale*, roughly "a mortar of pig's meat." Hey, no baloney.

In its pallid American versions (i.e., baloney, bologna), the *mortadella* of ancient, noble lineage has become one of the lowliest of the sausages, along with the hot dog, derived from respected European prototypes—the worst of the wurst. As a consequence, it has been relegated in figures of speech to that lower order of animal-derived foods which also has made pejorative terms of tripe and chopped (chicken) liver. Baloney probably earned the dubious distinction because it has been one of the very cheapest acceptable sources of animal protein during hard times. (In a haunting, indelible childhood memory of the Great Depression, a gaunt sharecropper in threadbare overalls enters a general store in back-country Georgia, reluctantly slips a dime onto the counter and requests "three cents' worth of crackers [sold loose from a barrel] and seven of baloney," while a wife and three kids straight out of a Walker Evans photograph wait for lunch in a jalopy parked outside by the gas pump. Relatively oblivious of real hardship as I still was then, I abruptly lost my taste for the nickel bottle of Dr. Pepper I was sucking on.)

Tripe was and remains something that the overwhelming majority of Brits and Yanks would starve before they'd eat, and hence for them it is easily equated with worthlessness, however it may be venerated in Normandy. Chopped liver's relatively recent entry into this exclusive company is more problematic. As a metaphor for insignificance, it could have come only from the Borscht Belt or some other venue frequented by American Jews—venues where the stuff is no less revered and no less a part of folklore than *foie gras* in Burgundy. The guess here is that because chopped liver never is served as anything but an appetizer, its status relative to that of the main course of a meal is the equivalent of a second banana's in a stand-up comedy routine, or a forgettable act sacrificed at the start of a show, to keep the natives from getting restless while the headliners still are putting on their makeup.

To anyone as long in the tooth as the more unfortunate among us may be, "vanilla" as a metaphor for wussiness ("a vanilla personality") is incomprehensible. Even in its present synthetically debased state, vanilla is perennially by far the most popular ice cream flavor, outselling the place and show finishers, chocolate and strawberry, combined. For those of us who predate the baby boom generation, genuine vanilla is a sensory tattoo that will accompany us to our graves; it's unexpungeably a memory of our skins and taste buds and nasal passages: a flavor and scent poignantly evocative of small-town, slow-paced America, which Norman Rockwell strove to capture. To enter an ice cream parlor or soda fountain before the late 1950s was to immerse oneself in a sweet cleanliness, a wicked innocence, the most antiseptically seductive sensory experience that life had to offer. The heady bouquet of real vanilla was an amalgam of innocence and experience that left prepubescent kids yearning for nothing they could put a label to; it broke your heart before you knew you had one. It was the diametrical opposite of the blandness with which it's associated today.

Folk etymology is the accepted term for the misattribution of words or phrases, either through misreadings of earlier coinages or through superficial "logic" that on closer analysis turns out to be wide of the mark. The generally accepted notion, discussed earlier, that "barbecue" derives from the French *de la barbe à la queue* is a classic example of misguided folk etymology, as are the opportunistic ascription of "rosemary" to "rose of Mary" and similar misperceptions.

Folk etymology likewise bestows credit where it isn't due in the term "Jordan almond." Neither the nut itself nor the popular confection of the same name has anything to do with the Hashemite Arabic kingdom or the river that it shares with Israel. Almonds are the products of a small tree, *Prunus amygdalus*, literally "tonsil plum," indigenous to the western Mediterranean. The so-called Jordan almond is simply a larger-than-ordinary specimen of the breed, grown in Spain (more specifically around Málaga, where the soil and climate seem to be particularly conducive to healthy development).

Prized throughout Europe during the Middle Ages, the Spanish import was termed *jardin* ("garden") *almande* (or *almande de jardin*) in Old French, whence it seeped into Middle English with unchanged spelling. Modern English, as we've already seen, doesn't easily assimilate foreign terms with no modification, especially when near-homonyms (e.g., "Jerusalem" for *girasole*) are ready to hand. Hence "Jordan" for *jardin*, the latter originally used in the same sense as "orchard," to differentiate between selectively cultivated almonds and their runtier, probably less flavorful and aromatic wild counterparts.

English culinary terminology later would play similar games, some of them willfully insouciant, with all manner of established alien nomenclature. *Imam bayeldi*, for example, was the standard designation throughout much of the Islamic world for a widely eaten eggplant dish. Its Arabic name, meaning "the priest fainted," is anecdotal: A certain imam, or spiritual leader, is supposed to have passed out from sheer rapture on tasting it for the first time. As the Ayatollah Khomenei and others recently have demonstrated, imams can become political as well as spiritual leaders. Still, a political ruler in the Islamic world isn't necessarily, or often, an imam. A sultan, for example, is an absolute ruler (the word is from the Aramaic *shutānā*, "power"), but his title implies no particular religiosity other than pro forma adherence to the Moslem faith. More inclined toward alliteration than accurate translation, British troops in the Middle East renamed the dish, making "sultan's swoon" of *imam bayeldi.*

As far as the remittance men from Blighty were concerned, a "wog" was a wog was a wog; anyone born east or south of the Strait of Dover qualified as such, and any term he or she might use was fair game for conversion to anything that could be made to sound even remotely English. And so the Hindi *catni* became "chutney," the Tamil *kari* became "curry," and another Tamil noun, *milagu-tanni(r)*, became "mulligatawny."

The term "alligator pear" as an alternative to "avocado" has been variously ascribed to the fruit's erroneously presumed prevalence in alligator-infested regions and to the roughness of its skin (although some varieties are notably smooth and shiny). The far more likely explanation is that "alligator" is nothing but a folk corruption of "avocado," perhaps coined euphemistically to divest the word of its testicular association (apart from its suggestive shape, it might be noted, the avocado grows in pairs). See you later, alligator. (The avocado, incidentally, also was known as "subaltern's butter" during the days when it was served, in lieu of the real McCoy, to junior ship's officers homeward bound from the Americas.)

As is well known, chop suey didn't originate in China, where the dish still doesn't exist, but in the United States, most likely in California. Its name derives via the Cantonese *tsap sui* from the Mandarin *tsa sui* ("mixed things"). The metamorphosis from *tsap* to "chop" was almost foreordained. Not only were both the American ear and tongue more comfortable with the latter, but a dish made up of *chopped* foods naturally evoked unwarranted etymological conclusions. Moreover, as an English verb, noun or adjective, "chop" had been associated for centuries with food, with the mouth (in one archaic sense, "to chop" was to take into the chops, or mouth, and eat) and with eating in general. *Sui* had no such associations to ease its passage into English. "Suey" was simply a mispronunciation, and there doubtless have been Americans who enunciated the Latin homonym the same way, as in "suey generis."

Chow mein, the other distinctively Chinese American dish which enjoyed widespread popularity before a growing awareness of authentic Chinese regional fare made both despised synonyms for gastronomic naïveté, takes its pidginized name from a Cantonese variant of the Mandarin *ch'ao* ("fried") *mein* ("noodles"). In this case, "chow," rather than having been influenced by preexisting English terms, spawned a new one: the American military designation for government-issue food of any sort, which later became the civilians' "chow down." (Both the breed of dog and chow-chow, the pickle relish, incidentally, have different Chinese antecedents.)

From a culinary and gastronomic standpoint, what goes around comes around. Chop suey and chow mein, both now considered infra dig by educated American diners, were the prototypes of the currently ultrachic, hybridized "Pacific Rim cuisine."

In seventeenth-century England, a "haricot" could be either a thick ragout, usually of mutton, or what's commonly termed the "string bean" or "French bean" nowadays. The legume, *Phaseolus vulgaris*, doubtless was introduced into England from France but almost as certainly was brought to France from Italy, sometime after the Italians acquired it from the Spaniards, who themselves had discovered it in Aztec Mexico. (The so-called French bean rightfully should be termed the Mexican bean, but, ironically, the only "bean" whose Mexican origin commonly is acknowledged in name isn't a true bean at all; it's the seed of certain shrubs of the genera *Sebastiana* and *Sapium,* which seed contains the live larva of a moth, *Laspeyresia saltitans,* and is known as the "Mexican jumping bean.") In English, both the ragout and the bean were appropriated intact from the French. In France, the ragout antedated the introduction of the bean, which might raise the question of why both wound up with the same label. The best scholarly speculation is that "haricot," the bean, may derive from the Aztec *ayacotl* or Nahuatl *ayecotli,* either of which could have been garbled to conform to a preexisting word.

When a bad egg of one sort or another gets his comeuppance, most people say he's received his "just desserts." Probably through some confusion between the sweetness of revenge and that of a meal's final course, they are in the wrong church and the wrong pew. The proper operative word is "deserts," with one *s,* and has no connection with food, except as a shark may be said to have a connection with a pilot fish. The nouns derive from different Old French roots that, like their respective descendants, were pronounced identically but had different spellings and meanings: *deservir* ("to deserve") and *desservir* ("to clear the table"). To compound the confusion, each connotes both punishment and reward:

deserts (usually plural) can be just as "just" for saints as sinners, while children who eat their spinach or don't can expect dessert (usually singular if their parents know what's good for them) to be served or withheld accordingly. In its literal sense, "just desserts" would be an appropriate slogan for a pastry shop or an ice cream parlor but doesn't apply to a parking ticket or a hanging. The vagaries of language being what they are, however, the wages of sin (biblically singular) is widely perceived as pie à la mode.

"Pie à la mode" itself is a meaninglessly incomplete formulation, a sort of linguistic coitus interruptus that locks French and English in an awkward embrace without issue. In its legitimate usage, *à la mode* ("in the style") would be preceded by a French noun and followed by *de* ("of") and someone or someplace or other, as in *tripes à la mode de Caen, consommé à la madrilène,* etc. Whatever pie à la mode may be in the style of is anyone's guess, but before members of the French Academy get into a stew over the abuse of their language abroad, they might remember that one of the classics of their own culinary repertory goes by the equally meaningless name of *boeuf à la mode.* In the language of food, to paraphrase Lewis Carroll, a word or phrase would seem to mean whatever its user chooses it to mean.

If many foods have come by their names through the misuse of language, in one historic case misuse of language made a food of an American president. When John F. Kennedy, meaning to express his solidarity with the citizenry of Berlin, declaimed *"Ich bin ein Berliner!"* his ringing pronouncement fell on bemused German ears as "I am a jelly roll!" The term *"ein Berliner"* is short for *"ein Berliner Pfannkuche"*—a jam-filled pancake. To say what he meant, the president should have omitted the article.

In most cases, the garbling of food terminology has done violence only to language. On one sanguinary occasion, though, an inability on the part of one ethnic group properly to enunciate another's common food noun amounted to a death sentence. This was the infamous Sicilian Vespers of March 31, 1282, when suspected adherents of Charles I of Anjou were acquitted or condemned at trial on the evidence of their pronunciation of *cece*, the Italian for "chickpea."

CHAPTER 5

The Medium Is the Message

When a car festooned with ropes of lemons is parked outside an automobile dealership, the disgruntled purchaser's wordless message comes across loud and clear. There is no mistaking its precise meaning, and any attempt to verbalize it necessarily would weaken its impact; as an attention-getter, a sock in the eye beats a spluttered complaint every time.

One way and another, various foods and eating rituals have served as unvoiced means of communication since our remotest ancestors came down from the trees. The actual prototypes for the modern cartoonist's Neanderthalers may or may not have clubbed their prospective helpmates into submission and dragged them across the nuptial threshold by the hair, but it's a safe bet that they expressed an ethos, a claim to hierarchical status within the community and possibly even some dim stirrings of affection by using food as a form of tacit declaration. In his more tender or prideful moments, our old buddy Ugh may have offered Yurp, his mate and bearer of his Ughlets, a choice hunk of the day's kill as a token of his then otherwise inexpressible uxoriousness, or as a simple assertion of the prowess-derived social primacy he—and, by extension, Yurp—enjoyed. The vocabulary and grammatical structure may have been lacking, but the message was obvious: "Listen up, you parasitic slobs, you're eating tonight thanks to my spearsmanship, so my old lady gets first dibs—or second after yours truly, Numero Uno—on this rump of bison. You guys can make do with what's left."

In more advanced societies than Ugh and Yurp's, comestibles have been employed in lieu of words from classical antiquity down to the present. When young Greek males lobbed apples at the female objects of their affection, the unspoken message was "Marry me." Girls who caught the offerings tacitly assented to the proposals; the silent reply of those who deliberately muffed the tosses was "No way, creep." The delivery of Valentine chocolates today echoes the old Greek proposal: "Be [or, in the case of mated couples, continue to be] mine."

Decades ago in India, during some seasonal Hindu festival, I was powdered cap-à-pie with a multicolored cloud of aromatic spices flung at me by a laughing, winsomely spangled young woman. Obviously puzzled, I was informed by an English-speaking bystander that I was obligated by custom to marry the flinger. I could have done (and probably later did) worse, but the engagement was broken when I was shipped home before ever learning my fiancée's name.

From the dating teenagers' greaseburger-and-fries pig-out at the neighborhood junk food franchise to some old Peter Arno–type roué's tête-à-tête with a coeval's bimbo daughter at a big-ticket bastion of haute cuisine, the intimate sharing of meals is universally accepted as an overture to at least unilaterally anticipated amatory grapplings, perhaps most graphically spelled out in the notorious oyster-slurping scene from the movie version of Henry Fielding's *Tom Jones.*

Ritual foods—Easter eggs, hot cross buns, Christmas puddings, Chinese moon cakes, Passover matzohs and the like—obviously are, or once were, meant to convey at least a sense of generational continuity and familial respect for tradition, however obscured the underlying symbolism may have become with time. Southern Americans today may no longer realize that the black-eyed peas and collard greens they eat ritually at New Year's represent coins and currency, respectively, and their Mediterranean contemporaries may be equally ignorant of the similar significance of lentils at the same season, but both are at least vaguely aware that they are affirming and perpetuating something of value to ongoing communal stability. Everywhere in the world, certain foods are the unspoken metaphors for the joyousness or solemnity of certain important occasions. In almost every known culture, both the salient events of an individual lifetime—birth, coming of age, marriage, parenthood and death—and the major communal occasions, usually outgrowths of earlier pagan seasonal rites, are marked by ritual feasting.

Among the watershed transitions from cradle to grave, marriage probably has given rise to more forms of food-related expression than any other. At traditional Japanese Shinto wedding feasts, as we've already seen, the wedding itself ("the close association or union" in one standard dictionary definition) is symbolized by the ritual consumption of *hamaguri*, a clam broth, in the hope or expectation that, like the salient ingredient's valves, the bride and groom will achieve a perfect unison, a oneness made of two. It would be a bit churlish, one supposes, to point out to the happy celebrants that oneness perforce becomes twoness as cooking the broth opens and separates the clam's shells.

On the Istrian Peninsula, south of Trieste and populated chiefly by ethnic Italians and Croats, marriages traditionally are celebrated by the eating of a special pasta, *krafi*, and a festive cakelike bread called *treccia di pane all'ouva*, *treccia* meaning a braid or plait. Both dishes are uncommonly rich and elegant by relatively stolid regional standards, and both convey warm wishes for a sweetly prosperous union. *Krafi*, raviolilike dumplings, are served as an ordinary, savory mainland Italian pasta dish would be in the conventional progression of courses but easily could be mistaken by noninitiates for dessert. Their sweetness, derived from raisins, sugar and citrus zests, betokens marital bliss; their richness, a product of the immoderate use of eggs, cheese and rum (a nonindigenous, relatively pricey ingredient), signifies prosperity. The same elements figure largely in the traditional wedding bread recipe, with the same implications.

"Although not everyone in the nineteenth century could afford pasta at New Year's," writes Mary Taylor Simeti in *Pomp and Sustenance: Twenty-five Centuries of Sicilian Food*, "no sacrifice was too great to ensure that pasta was served at one's wedding breakfast." (Paradoxically, pasta today is considered one of the Western world's economy staples, macaroni-and-cheese being synonymous with American budget cookery of the 1950s, but was deemed a luxury food for centuries and a vehicle for scandalous overindulgence by Savonarola, who railed against fifteenth-century hedonists who flouted his notions of pious austerity by not only eating macaroni but eating it au gratin, instead of just plain boiled.)

Simeti goes on to say of the Sicilian wedding pasta, "Here too a certain type . . . was obligatory: *maccarruna di zitu* (*zitu* means fiancé in Sicilian) . . . served with a ragù of pork meat cooked with tomato sauce and, in some towns, *'ncaciata*—with pieces of cheese incorporated." While it lacks the sweetness and imported luxury ingredients of Istria's *krafi,* Simeti's recipe for *pasta 'ncaciata* is a sumptuously rich affair containing uncommonly generous quantities of mixed-meats, eggs, cheese, olive oil and optional salami, which, together with the macaroni itself, serve as metaphors for prosperity.

"Finances permitting," Simeti continues, "one could proceed to further courses at one's wedding breakfast, but all the pioneer ethnologists of the nineteenth century report that it was the pasta that made the party, and Carlo Levi bears witness to this tradition's having survived the Second World War":

> *I had climbed up to the villa, marvelous in its architecture and in the gardens high above the town in front of the sea, where the wedding banquet of one of the maid-servants was going on, with a flight of doves from the wedding cake, and dancing, and a dinner consisting, as was the custom, in one sole course of* pasta al forno *with*

a meat sauce, followed immediately by Jordan almonds,
cakes, almond crisps, beignets, colored desserts, macaroons,
chocolate rolls, lady fingers, Swiss pastries, and by an end-
less quantity of spumoni and cassatas, of ice cream molds
in chocolate and mocha, filled with hazelnut, with cream
and strawberry.

The *pasta al forno,* emblematic of prosperity, may have made the
party, but the message implicit in the itemized confections, pastries
and iced desserts was the assembled company's collective prayer for
a marital *dolce vita.*

In East Friesland, the pièce de résistance of a traditional wedding
feast, a huge ham, doesn't merely symbolize material prosperity but
makes a direct contribution to it. The ham remains uneaten during
the celebration and subsequently is sold by the newlyweds, who buy
a starter set of housewares with the proceeds.

In most cultures, certain foods or their customs of service are
used in lieu of embarrassing words to convey the hosts' esteem (genuine or feigned) for their guests and (genuine) themselves. In Egypt,
for example, it would be considered a mark of rudeness toward a
guest (and evidence of stinginess on the part of the host) merely to
fill a glass with tea. Etiquette (in any form an expression of respect)
requires generous overflow, with the spillage landing in a saucer.
Sloppy and cumbersome as the practice may be, its message is clear:
for you, honored guest, enough is not enough to convey my high
regard, nor is too much too much, either for you or the preservation
of my amour propre. As Margaret Visser and many others have

noted, travelers' tales are replete with horrified accounts of honored guests appalled by grotesque (by their lights) offerings intended as tokens of respect: sheep and fish eyes in Arabic communities and Japan, respectively, rabbits' heads in Provence and the like. Confronted with such ghastly tributes, the guest of honor either will politely decline the offering, thereby insulting the host, or tough it out, suck it up, turn green and shortly thereafter repair headlong to the nearest yawkitorium, where guts ignominiously will be spilled.

In my more squeamish younger days, I was invited to lunch with the proprietors of La Cigale, a small cafe in the Provençal city of Arles, outside which my family and I then were living. My hostess was a *pied noir*, a Frenchwoman who had emigrated to Algeria years earlier, plied her particular trade on the shadier pavements of Algiers, eventually opened a successful chain of whorehouses there and more recently fled back to France as the Algerian struggle for independence had made life somewhat parlous for colonials in North Africa. My host, her putative husband, was a slick-haired, involuntarily retired pimp. The main course was a rabbit stew, marvelously redolent of local herbs and garlic (the "vanilla of Provence"), with the joints and saddle artfully arranged around the beast's head. Flashing a mouthful of gold teeth, a chain of gold coins dangling in her ample cleavage, my hostess offered me the bunny's flayed and pop-eyed countenance as her expression of esteem for an American expatriate who had enriched her considerably during her Algerian absence, while her cafe was operated by an eminently respectable surrogate. To my everlasting mortification, I demurred, claiming an inordinate, altogether fictitious preference for rabbits' thighs, thereby evincing unseemly disregard for any feelings but my own. In my cowardice, I averted my eyes while she shrugged off my gaffe, gleefully scooped out the eyes of the rabbit and appreciatively munched them.

Without going to such anatomical extremes, the American host sounds the same message by offering Thanksgiving guests a choice of white meat or dark before family members are permitted to avail themselves of the same options. A popular decorative device of American interior design of the Federal period also expressed esteem for visitors through the medium of food—specifically pineapples— even when the actual fruit was unavailable. In Gracie Mansion, the New York City mayoral residence, for example, a frieze of molded-plaster pineapples offers a warm, if coded, welcome to guests who attend Hizzoner's official functions and less formal bashes. The symbolism goes back to the nation's early years, when the fruit was prone to spoilage during slow sea voyages from the West Indies. Those pineapples that survived shipment were prohibitively expensive and therefore reserved as expressions of esteem for particularly valued guests. Somewhere along the line, one supposes, it occurred to some frequent party-thrower that one-time use of a decorator and a plasterer was a lot cheaper in the long run than repeated purchases of the actual fruit. ("Pineapple," incidentally, is from *pinappel,* the Middle English word for today's "pine cone," to which the fruit of the tropical American plant *Ananas comosus* bears a superficial physical resemblance.)

Coded verbal messages involving foods and eating rituals can be as ambiguous or opaque to the noninitiate as can the substitution of actual or simulated edibles, or dining protocols, for the spoken word. As noted earlier, the Chinese who asks whether you have eaten is not inviting you to lunch but just passing the time of day. Similarly but less cordially, the Madison Avenue executive's parting shot after a casual street meeting, "Let's do lunch," isn't to be construed literally; translated, the message is a brusque "Don't call me, I'll call you."

At least since the earliest civilizations, the language of herbs has been the most highly codified (in every sense of *that* word) of the food-related means of communication. From pre-Hellenic times until the late eighteenth century, it was possible to "write" fairly elaborate wordless "letters" through the judicious composition of nosegays of mixed herbs. During a visit to Constantinople well along in the eighteenth century, according to Maggie Oster, the author of *Gifts and Crafts from the Garden*, the English poet and belletrist Lady Mary Wortley Montagu "learned of the amorous messages that Turkish women sent via flowers, the heritage of which can be traced to Persia, China, Assyria, and Egypt." Many, if not most, of the "flowers" in question were blossoming edible herbs. Oster goes on to point out, "Over the next century or so [which is to say, well into the Victorian era], a great variety of floral dictionaries were published, the best-known being Kate Greenaway's *Language of Flowers*."

As is apparent from Oster's remarks and from a goodly supply of old documentation, the language of flowers—edible herbs in particular and, to a lesser extent, spices—antedated the publication of floral dictionaries by millennia. The champions of the first Olympic games, for example, were crowned with laurel wreaths in commemoration of the Greek victory over the Persians at Marathon, in 490 B.C. Today we (or at least those of us who metaphorically have earned them) still look to or don't rest on our laurels, as the case may be, but the evergreen tree, *Laurus nobilis*, from sprigs of which the ancient victors' headgear were woven, still is known in Greece as the "Daphne tree." Daphne, as one of the earliest of the Greek myths goes, was so fetching a nymph that Apollo incessantly tried to hit on her, despite her disdain for his advances. When the horny sun god continued his sexual harassment without letup, more compassionate members of the pantheon spared fair Daphne further stalking by turning her into a laurel tree, apparently presuming she would prefer winding up as a salient ingredient of Maryland crab boil to winding up in the bed of a priapic oaf.

Laurel (a.k.a. "bay" today) also symbolized glory during the imperial Roman era, and legionnaires used it to clean bloodied weapons as a deterrent to any latent guilt pangs they may have harbored. The tree and its leaves were thought to be safeguards against lightning (Tiberius supposedly donned a laurel wreath and scuttled under his bed during electrical storms), but, on the downside, the death of a laurel was considered an ill omen and harbinger of death for humans. As Shakespeare put it in *Richard II*,

> 'Tis thought the king is dead; we will not stay.
> The bay trees in our country all are wither'd.

As action took a back seat to the life of the mind in ancient Greece
and Rome, the laurel wreath was transferred from the warrior's brow
to the poet's and the scholar's—an honor that survives in today's
"baccalaureate," derived directly from "laurel berry."

Fennel, the parsley family's *Foeniculum vulgare,* also has ancient
associations with the Battle of Marathon and, indeed, was termed
marathon in Greece, where it was an early symbol of success. (The
identification of both herbs with the battle site may have originated
in nothing more than their indigenous presence in the immediate
area.) Over the centuries, it has been used symbolically for various
purposes and to convey various messages. During the Middle Ages,
it was hung over doors (as were other herbs, individually or in combination) to inform evil spirits that they were no more welcome
than visiting mothers-in-law, and smeared on the teats of dairy live-
stock to deter malign forces from souring their milk. Later, blind
John Milton, rudderless among the udders, groped his way along as
best he could, following his nose:

> When from the boughs a savory odor blown,
> Grateful to appetite, more pleased my sense
> Than smell of sweetest fennel, or the teats
> Of ewe or goat, dropping with milk at even.

In sixteenth-century Italy, fennel was a readily recognizable symbol of flattery: *dare finocchio* was to—or attempt to—sweet-talk
someone's pants off. Earlier, the herb signified conquest of another

sort. According to Longfellow, for example, "He who battled and subdued / A wreath of fennel wore." Elsewhere in herbal lexicography, fennel is defined as "worthy of all praise."

Basil, other aspects of which were discussed earlier, still is worn in their hair by young swains in some parts of Italy, as a declaration of their marital intentions, and, depending on the context, can signify hatred, love or good wishes (its messages historically have been more ambiguous than any other herb's). Mistletoe (not a true herb and inedible as it may be) still earns a lip-lock from any member of the opposite sex found standing beneath it at Yuletide.

The language of herbs is now, alas, pretty much a dead one; borage (bluntness, courage), burnet (a merry heart) and hyssop (cleanliness, sacrifice) aren't likely to turn up on an obscure shelf at the rear of your local supermarket, behind the puppy chow and toilet cleansers, and the small, overpriced vials of dried rosemary or marjoram (blushes, joy, happiness) you *will* find there aren't precisely calculated to inspire romantic effusions. Until relatively recent times, however, while kitchen gardens remained amenities of ordinary life, a fresh sprig of this or that was fraught (a word that I, like the poet Robert Graves, am astonished to find myself using) with meaning for those privy to a green unspoken lingo whose relatively recent demise has divested life of a form of discourse more charming and fragrant than our own half-crippled verbalisms.

Until and during the heyday of the herbal dictionaries, edible plants served as a vocabulary for what otherwise was not readily expressible. In retrospect, there's a nostalgic, bucolic quaintness about the whole idea, an idealized notion of milkmaid or shepherdess purity, notwithstanding the distinct probability that the average milkmaid or shepherdess of yore stank to high heaven, was afflicted with various insect parasites and was likely to be in the family way without sanction of church, state or the community at large. Illiterate and ill-spoken, they largely depended for their communicative skills on an intimate knowledge of the plants that grew around them, and of those they made a language that later was adopted, more or less campily, by their social betters.

Inevitably, the herbal vocabulary shrank almost to the vanishing point in the West with increasing urbanization and the passage from use of everyday plants that theretofore had come readily to hand. How many of us today could even identify by sight, let alone decipher the messages of, say, angelica (inspiration), dock (patience) or blue salvia (I think of you)? And who today would attempt to compose a billet-doux of celery salt, freeze-dried onion flakes, factory-packaged "Italian seasonings" and the like?

At this cultural and temporal remove, it's all but impossible to puzzle out the nuances and syntax of the old herbal language. Many of the sentiments it expressed seem as trite today as a heart and paired initials carved on a tree trunk. Others often seem to overlap almost precisely, or to be generalized or contradictory almost to the point of meaninglessness, but they were readily understandable in their time to those conversant with their subtleties. Love may have been expressed by both mint and myrtle, for example (and somewhat more equivocally by basil, which also betokened hate in some circumstances), but what sort and degree of love did each connote? In the context of their times and in combination with other elements of the herbal vocabulary, the messages they carried doubtless were far more explicit than they now may seem.

The tacit connective parts of speech that made sense of the old floral means of expression have been lost over time, but the nouns and a few verbs survive. A sampling would include amaranth for immortality; borage (from the Arabic *abu rach*, or "father of sweat") for effort; caraway for faithfulness; celery for bad luck and death in ancient Rome; chervil, from the Greek *charéphyllon*, "herb of joy"; coriander for concealed merit; dandelion for oracle; hops for injustice; lavender for distrust, cleanliness, luck and devotion; lemon balm for sympathy; marjoram for blushes and joy; mint (probably depending on the particular variety) for virtue, love and passion; myrtle for two of the immediately foregoing three, not including virtue; nasturtium for patriotism.

Also, parsley for festivity (despite its associations since classical antiquity with death); pennyroyal for flight from danger; peppermint for warmth of feeling; rosemary for remembrance above all, but also for fidelity and loyalty; rue for virginity and its perhaps natural concomitant, sorrow, along with disdain, good health and long life; saffron for mirth; sage for domestic virtue, longevity, health and wisdom; sorrel for affection; sunflower for haughtiness; sweet alyssum for worth beyond beauty (backhanded compliment though it may have seemed to its recipients); sweet woodruff for cheerfulness and rejoicing; tansy as a declaration of war and for immortality (presumably the aggressor's); thyme for activity, happiness, courage and strength; violet for modesty (whence the surviving, verbalized "shrinking violet"); wormwood for absence and bitterness; yarrow for war; and zinnia for thoughts of absent friends.

It's no mere coincidence that various staple dried legumes and seeds have been equated with prosperity, fertility, good health and good fortune in a great many cultures. They are themselves eminently healthful, and good health connotes good fortune. The association with fertility is obvious, and the sheer numbers that make up a portion of any of these foods suggest a piling up of wealth that doesn't come readily to mind at the service of a single veal chop or slab of foie gras, the cost of either of which might keep a whole family in lentils for a month. The more rarefied viands of the bastions of haute cuisine may *require* wealth for their delectation, but they don't *symbolize* wealth for those who can afford them, or don't at the same gut level at which the lowly legumes and seeds do for those who are largely dependent on them for subsistence and might in a pinch sell their birthright for a mess of pottage.

Except in the cases of the few herbal maledictions already mentioned, the messages implicit in most foods are messages of reciprocal love, concern and esteem. Occasionally, however, foods are put to use as tacit expressions of belligerence or ad hominem contempt. One of the enduring images of the erstwhile silver screen is that of James Cagney smooshing a grapefruit into Mae Clarke's face, and a staple of slapstick comedy is the custard pie delivered spang onto someone's physiognomy. An occupational hazard of the politician's life is a pelting with rotten tomatoes or putrescent eggs, and a few restaurant waiters have been known or thought to lace sauces, soups and drinks, ordered by particularly irksome customers, with snot, spittle, diarrhetics or worse. (Unfounded as it may have been, a belief prevalent among Occidentals in Chinese restaurants a couple of generations ago was that the bodily emissions of chefly misanthropes went into the egg-drop soup.) To paraphrase Brillat-Savarin's best-known aphorism: Tell me what you are, and I won't tell you what you eat.

CHAPTER 6

Call Me Anything,
but Call Me for Dinner

The first time I ever found *alouettes sans têtes* ("larks without heads") on a menu, I took the term literally. That was back in the early 1960s, when my wife, small son and I were living in Provence, about ten kilometers outside Arles. We'd usually drive into town for the Wednesday and Saturday markets, then lunch either at La Cigale, the Alcazar (the subject of Van Gogh's *The Night Cafe*) or the Bar des Amis. Our shopping finished, we'd often stroll through town, working up an appetite between the late-morning closing of the market and the midday meal. It was just a few months into my first stay in France, and I still found myself looking askance at some of the delicacies displayed in the windows of the fancier food shops, particularly the whole roasted songbirds whose wire-thin legs culminated in pitiably curled little feet and whose seemingly reproach-

125

ful expressions killed my appetency for what otherwise looked like delectably browned morsels.

One Saturday, when the *plat du jour* at Bar des Amis turned out to be *alouettes sans têtes,* I naively decided to take the plunge; decapitated as described on the menu, the larks might be no more off-putting than the Sunday chicken. I was served a brace of veal rolls that left me feeling about as venturesome as if I'd ordered *braciola* in a Greenwich Village spaghetti house.

The lexicon of food is liberally larded with such figurative, often wry flights of fancy. A Venetian dish of ordinary kitchen oddments, for example, is called *polenta e oseleti scapai,* which translates loosely as "cornmeal with little birds that got away," and a Swabian specialty, *Ulmer Spatzen* ("Ulm sparrows") is a piece of birdless baked goods named in the same spirit. Usually sardonic, sometimes baselessly optimistic or snidely applied by outsiders to frugal regional specialties, such terms often are intended, like stand-up comedy, to take the sting out of hardship or deprivation, or to make the prosaic or unavoidable more palatable, if only in a wistful sort of way, usually through the mock aggrandizement of what's found lacking on the plate. Thus, we have "Scotch woodcock" for a dish of scrambled eggs and anchovies, "Scotch grouse" for tinned sardines and "Welsh rabbit" for a meltdown of cheese and beer conspicuously lacking in lagomorphic parts. ("A fancy culinary term," sniffs the American Heritage Dictionary in a passing reference to "Welsh rarebit," an apparently deliberate reformulation, coined around 1785, of the sixty-year-older original sarcasm.)

Unlikely as it may seem in view of the noble status and prohibitive cost of sturgeon today, the fish was generally despised in an earlier America, when it was taken in such numbers from the inland waters of the Eastern Seaboard that it had little market value, was eaten almost exclusively by the poor and facetiously was termed "Hudson River beef." (I've been unable to track down a similar contemporaneous euphemism for salmon, but there was such a glut of it on the New England market that it sold for a penny a pound when any takers were to be found and impelled prospective hired hands to stipulate as a condition of employment that they not be required to eat it more often than once a week.) Similarly, an overabundance of buffalo fish in the American South inspired the sobriquet "Mississippi turkey."

For reasons that now seem obscure, cod—as plentiful as sturgeon and salmon, although its procurement entailed more hardship and risk—was given more respect on the tables of New England and, indeed, became emblematic, along with beans ("Boston strawberries"), of regional gastronomy there. It was graded as "marchantable, middling and refuse" and in that order was exported to Catholic Europe, eaten at home and shipped to West Indian slaveowners under the name "Jamaica fish." (Despite the coincidentally orthographic and phonetic similarities, the term "scrod," applied to usually filleted young cod, is etymologically unrelated to the name of the adult fish—it also applies to young haddock—but derives ultimately from the Middle Dutch *schrode*, denoting a shred or slice.)

As it happens, fish traditionally has been a low-priority food among Americans in general, pork, chicken and, more recently, beef having been the animal proteins of choice, at least among butchers' meats. Proverbially, any light-fleshed food of relative unfamiliar-ity—rabbit, frogs' legs, rattlesnake and the like—"tastes like chicken" or some other species of domestic fowl. In their reluctance to face the fact that what's on their plates may be of piscatorial origin, Americans (and some others, mostly English speakers) have accounted in the zillions for canned tuna marketed as Chicken of the Sea and, on a much more limited scale, have begun to accept pricey, previously spurned blowfish tails only since they were re-christened "sea squab." Earlier, an East Indian salt-cured dried fish didn't find favor among members of the British raj until it was given the spurious label "Bombay duck."

In recent years, there has been an increasing tendency, with quasi-official approval in the English-speaking world, especially the United States, to cosmeticize many of the old, not particularly flattering names of various species of food fish. The anglerfish, for one, a par-ticularly ugly but uncommonly toothsome customer known in times less inclined toward euphemism as "monkfish" (for the cowllike sheath around its head), "frogfish," "sea devil" and "goosefish" (once again, fins of a feather flock together), now is marketed and featured on most restaurant menus under its neutral French designation, *lotte*. Similarly, an Australian species once known, descriptively enough, as "slimehead" has enjoyed a recent vogue in epicurean circles as "or-ange roughy," a term that doesn't have quite the same descriptive impact.

Occasionally, nomenclatural concessions are made to assuage conscience-stricken notions of truth-in-advertising. Hence, we have "mock turtle soup," the salient ingredient of which is a boiled calf's head, and the Berliner's *Falscher Hase* ("false hare"), a rather prosaic meat loaf as hareless as a billiard ball.

"Caviar" is a term that purists insist is applicable to the roe of the sturgeon and nothing else. Nonetheless, the deservedly less esteemed eggs of lumpfish, whitefish, salmon or just about anything else that sports scales and gills often are marketed under that label. The practice reached its reductio ad absurdam a few years ago, at the height of the unremitting nouvelle cuisine quest for esoteric comestibles that could be juxtaposed in uneasy relationships with other previously unheard-of ingredients. Ta da! onto the gastronomic scene came snail eggs, which made a fleeting appearance on some avant-garde menus as *caviar d'escargot* and were priced astronomically. (A gastropod mollusk an inch and a half in diameter necessarily yields a somewhat scantier number of comparably sized eggs than a gravid Caspian sturgeon, which can weigh in at better than three-quarters of a ton, 10 percent of which may be roe.) Nor is it absolutely required that eggs of *any* sort be in evidence when the term "caviar" is invoked. Various spinoffs of *baba ganoush*, a Middle Eastern purée consisting chiefly of roasted and mashed eggplant, appear on Western menus as "eggplant caviar," presumably because their suave textures combine with the vegetable's rich flavor and innumerable seeds to produce a palatal sensation remotely similar to that of the real McCoy.

Along with caviar, truffles and foie gras are synonymous with luxurious dining in the West. As with caviar, both have been invoked to glamorize or lend status to less exalted provender. To the so-called chocoholic, chocolate epitomizes gastronomic bliss, but the ultimate indulgence undergoes an exponential enhancement, at least conceptually, when a mere bonbon, explosive as its flavor may be, is termed a "chocolate truffle," with nothing but a deliberately contrived physical resemblance to the genuine article to justify the nomenclature. In Germany, a botanical misunderstanding that goes back to the introduction of the potato there has been perpetuated in the name of the lowly tuber: *Kartoffel,* which translates literally as "truffle."

Over the years, the term *foie gras* ("fat liver") has been put to more duplicitous uses, usually by makers of liver-based pâtés, mousses and purées. By French law, at least eighty percent of anything sold as *pâté de foie gras* must be specially fattened goose or duck liver but, as in the case of many another forcemeat preparation, legal requirements often have been evaded. The lawful specification for a mousse or purée of *foie gras* dwindles to a scanty 55 percent, lending the weight of constituted authority to what would be somewhat questionable labeling even were the law strictly observed. The label becomes altogether fraudulent, however, when used by a manufacturer willing to compromise the marginal integrity of his product by a mere 6 percent deviation from licit standards—a compromise made all too often by not-overly-fastidious pork butchers, especially in the provinces.

For many years and in several languages, leeks have been termed "poor man's asparagus." Again, what we have here is a relatively humble food wistfully aspiring to a more status-symbolic station. Or *had;* ironically, the current market cost of leeks, pound for pound, as they say in pugilistic circles, often is as great as, if not greater than, that of asparagus, and if present economic trends continue, the latter soon may become the former's "poor man's" option. In Wales, of course, the leek has enjoyed noble status for centuries and was worn on their helmets by the Welsh soldiery, both as an identifying badge and a protective talisman. In Shakespeare's *Henry V*, the blustering English rogue infantryman Pistol cautions Welsh Captain Fluellen to "wear your leek about your head upon St. David's Day."

Those constrained by circumstances to eating humbler foods for want of better stuff haven't always been inclined to upgrade their nutrients with optimistic labels. The World War II GI, for example, sardonically dismissed the mess hall staple creamed chipped beef on toast as "shit on a shingle" (although many aging veterans now grudgingly confess to a nostalgic fondness for the dish). A great favorite of the Deep South goes by the unappetizing name "dirty rice," and an African subsistence seed, *acha*, is termed "hungry rice" by those dependent on it for survival. In Cuba, a shredded flank steak preparation (originally made with the meat of tough old goats hung on clotheslines to dry) goes by the unflattering name *ropa vieja*, or "old clothes." (Cuban food in general is nothing if not imagistic; another of the cuisine's classics, black beans and rice, is termed *moros y christianos*, "Moors and Christians.")

Speaking of rice, in one of the most drastic reversals of food-nomenclatural form a much rarer and pricier grain with much more distinctive characteristics, the seed of the northern American marsh grass *Zizania aquatica*, bears the name "wild rice," a botanical mis-

nomer and a nomenclatural comedown comparable to the misrep-
resentation of a Maserati as a Chevy Nova. ("Nova," incidentally,
was perhaps the most unfortunate name the manufacturer could
have come up with, at least insofar as the Latin American market
was concerned: In Spanish-speaking regions, the word was heard as
no va, "doesn't go." The language of food isn't the only one susceptible to winding up with egg on its face.)

   Countless foods throughout the world and throughout history
have sailed under false colors, usurping the names of others to which
they often have borne no kinship and little resemblance. To get a
bread-and-butter job out of the way first, in English alone we
have bread-and-butter pickles, breadfruit and *its* hand-me-down
Mexican breadfruit (monstera), sweetbreads, St. John's bread
(carob), breadnut (the fruit of the tropical American tree *Brosimum
alicastrum*), breadroot (a.k.a. "prairie turnip") and the Australian
"blackfellows' bread," a type of fungus eaten by aborigines. We also
have butternuts and, at a second remove, butternut squash, along
with butter beans, butter clams and butterfish, not to mention but-
ter-and-sugar corn, apple butter, peanut butter and butterhead lettuce.

   Elsewhere on the menu are beefsteak, cherry and plum tomatoes;
muttonfish, which is neither mutton nor fish but abalone in Australia; custard apples, which are neither custard nor apples; oyster
mushrooms and oyster plant (salsify); turtle beans, kidney beans,
sea beans (samphire), marrow beans and asparagus beans; partridge
sole, lemon sole, chicken halibut, mutton snapper and the sunfish
known as "pumpkinseed"; hen-of-the-woods mushrooms, "Mexican potatoes" (jicama) and a type of rockfish called "chilipepper,"

along with Chinese gooseberry (kiwi fruit, botanically unrelated to true gooseberries), eggplant, rhubarb chard, "candy cane" (the Chioggia beet), soy milk, coconut milk, spaghetti squash and "tree tomato" (tamarillo). The ancient Persians termed the apricot "egg of the sun," and slightly less ancient New Yorkers nostalgically recall the "egg cream," a soda fountain concoction devoid of both its nominal ingredients.

Occasionally, a term will take on a spurious meaning only because a regional accent has been misheard by other speakers of the same language. As a case in point, *Aalsuppe*, a specialty of Schleswig-Holstein, translates literally as "eel soup," although eel didn't originally appear in the dish. Here is Horst Scharfenberg, the author of *The Cuisines of Germany*, on the subject:

> **Aalsuppe,** *the distinctive festive dish of the Hanseatic Free City of Hamburg, sounds like it should mean "eel soup," since* Aal *is the German word for eel. However, the people of Hamburg and neighboring Holstein, like Bostonians in the United States, are renowned for the broadness of their* a*'s, and* aal *(pronounced something like "awl") is the northern German way of saying* alles, *"all" or "everything." And so,* Aalsuppe *is a soup (originally a stew) that has everything. Eventually, perhaps due to the workings of folk etymology,* alles *came to include an eel or two, since these creatures are quite common in the rivers of Holstein.*

It's abundantly evident from the recipe Schafenberg provides that *Aalsuppe* indeed "has everything." He lists no fewer than thirty-five ingredients, several made up of multiple elements, and while he includes an optional two pounds of eel, presumably for the benefit of literalists, the dish would include damn near everything edible, even were its seemingly indispensable ingredient omitted Aaltogether.

And so it goes within the broad, infinitely flexible parameters of the language of food. Ironies abound, as do tin-eared adaptations of alien terms, wrongheaded folk etymology, oxymoronic constructions, botanical and icthyological misperceptions, wildly inaccurate notions of provenance, labels based on nothing more logical than ethnic or regional bias and all the misguided rest of it. Still, the language of food remains the most elemental, vital and colorful language we have and accounts for mythic, folkloric and metaphorical dimensions without which our speech and literature would be impoverished indeed.

To wrap up this by no means exhaustive survey, what other language could manage to confuse two primary colors, as when the English "red cabbage" and German *Blaukraut,* or "blue cabbage," turn out to be one and the same member of the family Brassica? What other would impel the French, notable consumers of green beans, to indict themselves by nicknaming their beloved *haricots verts* "rascal stuffers"? Or persuade Italians to christen a dessert that's neither a soup nor English *zuppa inglese*? In what other language but the language of food would the cayor apple of Senegal become the "gingerbread plum," carrots in Ireland be termed "underground honey" or the tails of beavers officially be sanctioned as fish in

Poland during Lent, because most of their time is spent underwater? Where else outside the language of food will you find an equivalent term for the "mountain chicken" applied to a species of toad eaten on some Caribbean islands, where the local bonefish is termed "banana fish"?

In the cowboy lingo of the American southwest, pinto beans are "Mexican strawberries," although conventional strawberries aren't true berries at all, as tomatoes are. The conger eel once was termed *Belle-Île boeuf* ("beef") in France, the crappie is *sac-à-lait* ("milk bag") in Cajun Louisiana, and chives are *Schnittlauch* ("the cuttable leek") in Germany. Also in Germany, genuine truffles (as opposed to potatoes usurping the name) are referred to as "ground pears." (The ovoid fruits of various cacti of the genus *Opunta*, termed "prickly pears," have about as much to do with true pears as the peach, once termed "Persian apple," has to do with the true apple.) The "water chestnut" of China and Southeast Asia isn't, of course, a chestnut by any botanical definition, nor is either of two marine food fishes, *Coryphena hippurus* and *C. equistus*, a dolphin, although both went by that name until a few years ago, when it was superseded by the Hawaiian term *mahi mahi*, in a public relations gesture, as concern for the welfare of the anthropomorphically lovable aquatic mammal became an ecological priority.

The pork butcher's product called "head cheese" obviously isn't cheese by any stretch of the imagination—unless the etymology of "cheese" in the Romance languages is traced back to its ultimate source, the Greek *formos*, whence the Italian *formaggio* and French *fromage* derive. Like most true cheeses, head cheese is *formed* in a mold of some sort (as noted earlier, the original *formos* was a wicker basket), hence the French *fromage de tête* and our own "head cheese." The Italian term for the same preparation, incidentally, is *coppa* (a "bowl" or "cup"), which also refers to the molds in which a highly gelatinous mixture took shape as it cooled and solidified.

Of the several broad categories of foods, none has generated as much nomenclatural confusion as the marine and freshwater comestibles, the common names for which may vary from region to region. The Delmarva Peninsula's "rockfish," for example, is "striped bass" elsewhere, while "snapper" may designate any of numerous members of the family Lutjanidae in various parts of the English-speaking world but is applied to an entirely unrelated species, the bluefish, *Pomatomos saltatrix,* on the East End of Long Island (New York), as well as to a particular growth stage: prepubescence.

Terminology may not only vary from region to region, as in the case of mussels in Italy, but from elbow to elbow, as in Barcelona's central market, the Mercado de San José (more familiarly, La Boquinera), where identical species of shellfish sold from neighboring stalls bear altogether different labels. One type of Mediterranean murex, *Murex brandaris,* for one, is offered as *caracoles* by one vendor, while a retailer at her elbow displays land snails under the same name and others nearby hawk the same marine gastropods as *canarillas.* Similarly, several diminutive bivalves of the family Tellinidae, one indistinguishable from another except by an experienced conchologist, bear such names as *rosellana* and *tallina,* depending on whom you're doing business with.

The term "devilfish" has been conferred on so many unrelated ugly customers of the marine world—among others, various octopi, rays (a.k.a. "skate," "manta"), the anglerfish (a.k.a. just about anything you choose to call it), the indispensable ingredient of bouillabaisse known in France as *rascasse* and its western Atlantic relative, the sculpin; indeed, almost any piscatorial critter of less-than-comely appearance—that it has been rendered meaningless through overuse. Ugliness, as well as beauty, is in the eye of the beholder, and who's to say that the male octopus we find grotesque doesn't set the female's heart aflutter or vice versa?

Foodspeak changes with advances in food technology. Today's "smelt," a reversion to the Middle English term for freshwater or marine members of the family Osmeridae, was yesterday's "candlefish," so named for its extreme fattiness, which enabled bygone generations to dimly illuminate what was on their dinner plates by threading a wick lengthwise through the fish and lighting it. To add to the general confusion, we have such apparent oxymorons as "salmon trout" and "mackerel shark," the latter including the eminently toothsome mako and the forbiddingly toothy great white of *Jaws* notoriety.

And so we muddle along, dogged by imprecision but reveling in the exuberance of a language that still retains its bumptious naïveté. Who cares, finally, whether "Peruvian carrot" turns out to be a double misnomer for arracacha (who knows what in the world arracacha *is*?), or that "tea melon" (a variety of sweet cucumber) has nothing to do with either tea or melons, or that "corn salad" (a.k.a. "field salad," "lamb's lettuce," "lamb's tongue" and, more salably these days, *mâche*) has nothing to do with corn, either in "corn's" generic association with various grains or the more specifically American *Zea mays*?

Whatever it may be called, eat what's on your plate and be thankful for it. With a little bad luck, you, instead of your former neighbor, might be sleeping, foodless, on a hot-air vent on Madison Avenue, within drooling distance of Caviarteria.

Chewing the Fat

The scene is a neighborhood saloon during the dog days of summer. Lou, a regular sort of meat-and-potatoes guy, has just ordered his second brewskie when his buddy Phil joins him at the bar.

LOU: Hey, what's cookin'?

PHIL: Ah, I'm really fed up. (*to the bartender*) Mike, lemme have a vodka martini, straight up, no fruit.

LOU: Jeez, what's eating you? You never hit the hard sauce unless you're really steamed.

PHIL: It's that goddamn Grabowski. The used car guy? You know him. Smooth as butter and slippery as an eel. Full of crap as a Christmas turkey. Handshake dead as a lox. Bastard takes me for a real meatball and I fork over two thousand clams—a lot of bread when three kids are eating me out of house and home—for what turns out to be this goddamn lemon that ain't worth a hill of beans. Damn thing's been to the shop three times in the month I've had it. Costing me dough like there's no tomorrow and left me flat as a pancake. (*to bartender*) Hey, Mike, the same again and another Bud for Lou. Put 'em on my tab.

LOU: Hey, take it easy, big guy. You don't wanna get stewed.

PHIL: Ah, what's the difference? I'm not gonna get a deewee with a car that don't even run. Hell, I've been so mad I've been marinating myself in this stuff since that . . .

LOU: That bad, huh?

PHIL: Yeah, you betcha it's that bad. Really tough to swallow. The old lady's been chewing me out about it every time I come home to tie on the feedbag since this bastard fed me this line of baloney about how this total wreck was the greatest thing since sliced bread. I'll tell you, I've really had a bellyful with that turkey. Went out and got myself so pie-eyed last night that I wind up popping my cookies like a goddamn pizza-faced teenager.

LOU: Hey, man, simmer down. You could give yourself a stroke in weather like this.

PHIL: Yeah, jeez, you could fry eggs on the sidewalk on a day like this. I mean, it's really broiling out there.

LOU: What's wrong with the car?

PHIL: What *isn't*? You name it, everything from soup to nuts.

First thing I find out is the radiator's full of holes as a Swiss cheese. Ah, forget about it. The damn thing just no way cuts the mustard.

LOU: (*changing the subject*) You heard about Ralph?

PHIL: Which Ralph? Ralph the Stringbean or Jelly-belly Ralph?

LOU: Jelly-belly. Lard-ass. Seems he's in a real pickle these days. Got behind in his child support and his old lady really stuck it to him. Skewered him like shish kebab and landed him in the soup in family court.

PHIL: How'd he let something like that happen? With the kind of cabbage that guy's taking down, we're talkin' small potatoes.

LOU: Yeah, well, it's a *hot* potato now. He thought his case was a piece of cake. Tried to butter up the judge and really made a hash of it. Came up with a bunch of half-baked excuses and got eaten alive. Judge chewed his ass out like it was sirloin steak. Nailed him like a sitting duck and made dead meat out of him. Told him he'd have to eat the whole nut by next week or his ass'd be in the deep-freeze when everyone else got up from the table. Old Ralph, he tried to strike a deal with LaVerne, but she told him to go pound salt.

PHIL: LaVerne? Jeez, butter didn't melt in her mouth when she was younger. Remember her in high school? She was quite a dish, but she's no spring chicken anymore.

LOU: Yeah, she was a good-looking tomato, but not exactly

my cup of tea. She had a kind of white-bread, cookie-cutter personality that didn't go with her looks.

PHIL: Well, I wouldna minded getting my meat hooks into her, but I was working for her father after school and had a pretty good idea which side my bread was buttered on. I mean, that after-hours gig was my meal ticket in those days, and I figured if it came down to my job or his daughter, half a loaf was better than none. Besides, her daddy was a real good egg, salt of the earth, and I didn't want him giving me the fish eye. Anyway, LaVerne was sort of pea-brained and we wouldna hit it off exactly like ham and eggs.

LOU: Yeah, I don't think you would have. LaVerne always had popcorn for brains, but when she married Ralph they seemed in some ways like two peas in a pod. He'd always been in hot water, but he went straight from the frying pan into the fire when he married her.

PHIL: Yeah, man, you said a mouthful there. She seemed like a cream puff in those days, but I guess old Ralph found out he'd bit off more than he could chew.

LOU: Well, Ralph was so hungry for a piece of cherry pie he was lost in a pea-soup fog back then. LaVerne came on to him sweet as sugar, and, like they say, honey draws more flies than vinegar.

PHIL: Yeah, but you can't make an omelet without breaking eggs, and it looks like they broke a crateful before they finally split up. Now, the icing on LaVerne's cake is this child support judgment.

LOU: Listen, you hungry? Why don't we go to the Chinese joint for a bite to eat?

PHIL: (*to bartender*) Hey, Mike, give us another round and then we're gonna get something to eat.

MIKE: I thought you just did.

Part 2

Alphabet Soup:

A GLOSSARY

*T*he intent here is not to define food words and eating-related terms in their primary, usually self-evident usages, except in those cases that may be unfamiliar or obscure to the general reader. It would be an insult to anyone's intelligence, in the context of this book, to provide primary definitions of such common nouns as, say, "milk," "bread," "butter" and the like, but the etymology of such staple terms may be of interest, as may their metaphorical and symbolic applications (familiar though some of them may be) as reminders of the pervasive influence of food terminology on language in general and, conversely, of the widespread seepage into foodspeak by less specifically directed words, phrases and expressions.

The structure used here is nonrigid and largely reflects subjective priorities. The content is selective, not encyclopedic, and etymological data may precede or follow factual or speculative information, without much regard to conventional form, while any incidental notions or conceits that come to mind may be included. In short, the lexicography

147

is informally presented but has been made as accurate as possible, given a reasonably well informed layman's limitations. Where etymological discrepancies are not specified, the preponderance of authoritative opinion has been relied on.

ᛏᛏᛏᛏᛏᛏᛏᛏᛏᛏᛏᛏᛏᛏ

A

aardvark. A burrowing mammal, *Orycteropus afer*, of southern Aafrica, occasionally eaten by aaborginals. From the obsolete Aafrikaans for "earth-pig." The critter doesn't much indulge in aabalone, aalbacore, aaples or aasparagus but feeds largely on aants.

abalone. A marine univalve gastropod of the genus *Haliotis*. From New World Spanish *abulón*. Also known as ormer and *ormeau* on the English and French sides of the channel, respectively; *oreille de Saint-Pierre* ("St. Peter's ear") along the French Mediterranean coast; *awabi* in Japan; *paua* among the Maori of New Zealand; "muttonfish" in Australia; etc.

albacore (*Thunnus alalunga*). The generally preferred source of canned tuna, its English name ultimately derives via the Portuguese *albacor* from the Arabic *al-bakrah* ("the young camel"), the latter presumably from a resemblance of sorts between the flesh of both creatures.

allspice. The dried unripe berry of the tree *Pimenta dioica* takes its common English name from its commingling of the flavors of cinnamon, nutmeg and clove. Like vanilla and flakes and powders derived from various capsicum peppers, it's one of the three spices in widespread use native to the Western Hemisphere. Botanical confusion abounds in most languages, with the berry variously identified as a pimento (in Spanish, French, Portuguese, German and Dutch) and the unrelated peppercorn in Swedish (*kryddpeppar*) and Italian (*pepe di Giamaica*). The English term, in somewhat mangled form, is used elsewhere only in Japan, where an attempted phonetic rendering has produced *ôrusupaisu.*

almond. The nut of the tree *Prunus amygdalus,* native to the Mediterranean region and known to the Romans of classical antiquity as the "Greek nut." The modern noun is descended from the Greek *amugdalē.*

   almond-eyed. Having eyes shaped like almonds. A characteristic mostly applied to Asian females, although it is no less applicable to Asian males.

anchovy. Any of various small, herringlike marine fishes of the family Engraulidae. From the Spanish *anchova, anchoa,* which latter may derive from the Basque *anchu.*

anchovy pear. The mangolike fruit of the tropical American tree *Grias cauliflora.* One of innumerable foods whose popular names derive from resemblances of one sort or another to unrelated edibles (e.g., breadfruit, cranberry bean, beefsteak tomato, muttonfish), the anchovy pear is so called because, like its eponym, it usually is served as an hors d'oeuvre.

angel food. 1920s American hobo slang for the mission house ser-
mon that had to be endured by the recipients of free eats.

angler fish, anglerfish. Any of various deepwater marine fishes of
the order Lophiiformes, or Pediculati, equipped with an attenuated
dorsal fin ray that extends forward over the mouth, as a lure to
attract prey. It's unlikely that you'll ever find a compleat angler at
the fishmonger's, because the critter's strikingly uncomely physiognomy is considered a deterrent to sales and usually is removed
and discarded prior to display. Also known as monkfish, for the
cowled appearance of its head; toadfish (French *crapaud*), in tribute
to its ugliness; devil fish or sea devil (*diable de mer*); goosefish, possibly for the richness of its flesh; and bellyfish; but often listed on
restaurant menus as the less negatively evocative *lotte.*

anise, anise seed, aniseed. The aromatic seed of the herb *Pimpi-
nella anisum,* a member of the parsley family indigenous to Asia
Minor, the Greek islands and Egypt. In ancient Greece, no nomenclatural distinction apparently was drawn between anise and its close
botanical kinsfellow dill (*Anethum graveolens*), and the same noun,
anison, indiscriminately was applied to both, with some later confusion resultant. The more precise Romans used the distinct terms
anisum and *anēthum,* and their word for anise survives essentially
intact in most modern languages: *anis* in Spanish, French, German,
Russian and Swedish; *anijs* in Dutch; *anice* in Italian; *anisu* in Japanese; *yānîsūn* in Arabic. A salient exception is the Portuguese *erva-
doce* ("sweet herb").

antipasto. Although more than one food writer has translated the

Italian term as "before the pasta," its literal meaning is "before the meal."

apee. A soft sugar-and-sour-cream cookie created in Philadelphia by the nineteenth-century cook Ann Page, from whose initials the term derives.

apple. In addition to the various symbolic applications and slang usages discussed on pp. 14–15, a saddle horn was termed "the apple" by old-time cowboys, and the fruit also has been used to designate a baseball ("the old apple"). A fellow or chap may be "a good apple" or "a bad apple," and one of the latter in a crowd of the former metaphorically spoils a heavily populated barrel. In a proverbial formula for good health, one a day is believed to keep the doctor away.

  apple, alley. 1. A cobblestone. **2.** A horse turd.

  apple butter. An old American slang term for smooth talk.

  apple, Satan's. Mandrake (*Mandragora officinarum*), which according to folklore emits a shriek when uprooted "that none might hear and live." Magical properties long have been attributed to the plant, but not, as noted by John Donne, the ability to bear human children.

  apple pie. What almost nothing putatively is more American than, especially if baked by Mom, its European origins notwithstanding.

  apple pie order, in. The expression, indicative of tidiness, precise functionalism, impeccable maintenance and the like, generally is believed to be a corruption of the French phrase *nappe pliée en ordre*, "linen folded in an orderly fashion." No convincing refutation has turned up yet.

apple polisher. One seeking to curry favor, as schoolchildren once did by presenting teachers with apples polished on their sleeves. Later equivalents, with no food-derived connotations, are "brown-noser" and "ass-kisser." "Boot-licker" predated both in common usage.

applesauce. What those today who are full of scatological matter were full of in a more genteel era. "Baloney" was then synonymous.

apples, little green. Any dead certainty is as sure as God made 'em.

apricot. See p. 9.

artichoke. See p. 9.

asparagus. A.k.a. "speargrass" in some regional dialects.

aspic. See p. 36.

avocado. See p. 16.

B

bacon. 1. What the family breadwinner(s) bring(s) home (p. 45). **2.** With "one's," what is saved when one is delivered from a precarious situation, a possible euphemism for "saved one's ass."

bagel. The name of the hard-boiled doughnut of Eastern European Jewish cookery made its way to its present form from the Yiddish *beygel,* derived successively from the Middle High German *Bouc* and the Old High German *Boug,* both denoting a ring or bracelet.

Although the bagel had transcended its parochial ethnic origins by the early 1980s to take its place as both an international weekend brunch staple (see p. 41) and the degraded basic component of several snack-food products, it remains symbolic—at least for those who take a proprietary interest in it—of the gastronomic naïveté and cultural otherness of those not to the manner born. As one of innumerable bagel-based jokes has it, a group of visiting Texas "bidnessmen" drop into a New York Jewish deli one morning. In the midst of their breakfast, they peremptorily summon the proprietor, who approaches their table in edgy anticipation of a complaint of some sort. "Oh, no," he's assured. "Evathang's jes' fahn. But tell us, which of these thangs are the bagels and which are the loxes?"

bagna cauda. Literally "hot bath," a popular Piedmontese dipping sauce of olive oil or butter, pulverized anchovies and garlic, served with raw vegetables as an appetizer.

bain-marie. The French term, in widespread English use, for a double boiler. Originally *bain de Marie* ("Mary's bath"), an alchemist's utensil supposedly named for Moses's sister, an alchemist. In culinary usage, the eponymous Mary is believed by some to be the Virgin, whose gentle nature is reflected in the mildness of the cooking process.

baker's dozen. Originally a dozen loaves or other pieces of baked goods plus one "for good measure"; a self-protective device adopted by English bakers after 1266, when bread was sold by weight, vendors' scales were unreliable and new consumer protection laws were harshly enforced. The practice of adding a thirteenth unit to a round dozen gradually was adopted by other foodsellers and still is observed in such traditional venues as the open markets of Europe, where, say, a "dozen" eggs usually nets the purchaser thirteen, and where a bit more than was stipulated often is added to foods sold by weight. The custom of sticking an extra candle into a birthday cake ("and one to grow on") probably was spun off from the "one for good measure" of the baker's dozen.

balsamic vinegar. Italian *aceto balsamico.* The slowly aged specialty of Modena, Italy, is widely believed to have medicinal value and takes its name from the Latin *balsamum* ("balm").

banana. The word, of West or Central African origin, made its way into various European languages via the Spanish and Portuguese. The earliest known published reference (to the "bonano") in English occurred in 1697. American police argot for an unreliable informer, a small-time free-lance criminal or a nonentity in an organized crime ring.

banana-nosed. Having a prominent hooked proboscis.

banana peel. A perennial symbol, in popular art and literature, of misadventure lying in wait for unsuspecting victims, an accident about to happen.

bananas. Crazy, NUTS. Probably from the antics of monkeys.

banana stick. See p. 65.

banana, top. The headliner of a theatrical revue, or the more prominent member of a comedy duo.

banger. See p. 61.

barbecue. See p. 28.

bard. To tie strips or sheets of fat around lean meats or fowl to prevent dryness during roasting. The verb's original meaning had to do with protectively blanketing or padding a warhorse and derives ultimately from the Arabic noun *barda'ah*, a stuffed packsaddle.

barleycorn. The seed or grain of the cereal grass barley, *Hordeum vulgare*, used in the ancient world as a unit of measure.

Barleycorn, John. The personification of malt liquor or hard booze, invoked by American prohibitionists as evil incarnate.

Bartlett pear. A pear developed in eighteenth-century England and introduced into Massachusetts by Enoch Bartlett.

basil. See pp. 33, 120.

basmati rice. A long-grain East Indian rice grown in the foothills of the Himalayas and renowned for the seductiveness of its aroma. The Indian word *basmati* means "queen of fragrance."

batter. See p. 66.

battery acid. Mess hall coffee in the parlance of World War II GIs.

bean(s). As one of the world's primary staple foods, beans of one sort or another have been invoked throughout history as symbols, metaphors and the like, to cover a range of subjects that includes just about anything concerned with human affairs, traits, attitudes, perceived otherness, etc. As noted on p. 50, Tuscans and Bostonians are mildly denigrated as "beaneaters," an appellation also used, somewhat more contemptuously, in reference to indigenous Mexicans, especially of the poorer classes. Similarly, citizens of Leicester, England, historically have been termed "beanbellies" in neighboring regions where their dietary preferences aren't shared.

In one context or construction or another, the word "bean" is applied, mostly with jocular affection but sometimes pejoratively, both to people themselves and to the various traits, proclivities and physical attributes associated with them, especially in English. In Britain and, to a lesser extent, the former British colonies, for example, "old bean" long has been an affectionate term of address for upper-class males, and "the old bean" is the human head and its intellectual capacities. The working-class equivalent in England, also food-derived, is "loaf," as in "Use your bloody loaf, mate."

Beans are "money" in several languages and symbolize money in many rituals, and people who are flat broke "haven't got a bean." Beans are about which someone unacquainted with a particular subject doesn't know; the expression possibly originated in nineteenth-century Boston, where an education was deemed incomplete without thorough familiarity with the baking of beans, but may derive from "knowing how many beans make five," from an early English exercise in which small children being taught simple arithmetic used beans as counters.

bean counter. An accountant or, by extension, anyone occupied with precise quantification or prissy exactitude of any sort. Possibly from the aforementioned children's exercise.

beanery. An eating establishment of no particular distinction.

beanfest. A church supper (also "bean supper") or similar event at which bean dishes are featured.

beanpole. A tall, lanky person; a "stringbean."

bean ray. A ship's pennant, flown at mealtimes to indicate that most of the vessel's complement is occupied at mess and unavailable for topside courtesies and obligations.

beans, full of. High-spirited or frisky, originally applied to farm animals fed largely on beans and thought to be livelier than others.

beans, hill of. What something of no value isn't worth. A "hill" of beans is a planting of four seeds or so around the base of a pole. A great many such hills will yield an appreciable food supply or cash crop, but an individual hill doesn't amount to much.

beans, spill the. To confess or yield evidence that incriminates oneself or others. Probably from a metaphor for vomiting.

Phaseolus Vulgaris Cano

Consider the string bean, *Phaseolus vulgaris*,
The *haricot vert* of the gourmands of Paris:

The pod that goes *pop*! when it's picked fresh and broken,
Known to some as the French bean (where English is spoken),
The green bean, the snap bean, "a tall skinny person."
(This ode won't get better—more likely, will worsen.)
The subject I've picked for this mismanaged ballad
Is one-third of the cast of a true three-bean salad.
In Florence, where diets are notably beany,
Real epicures dote on their *fagiolini.*
To the Cantonese, *been dau* (in transliteration)
Is prized when included in any collation.
In Valencia, string beans are *judias verdes,*
With leftovers eaten the second and third days.

From the jubilant ranks of the string bean's defenders
Omit Ogden Nash, who mixed species and genders,
Confessing he couldn't tell string bean from soy bean,
Admitting he couldn't tell a girl from a boy bean.
(On the island of Bali, the stupidest dunce is
Better informed on the bean he calls *buncis.*)
Nash was not of the bean's highest praises a singer;
Others were, and most notably farmer Stan Binger,
Whose name by sheer chance is an anagrammatic
Reworking of "string bean." (Please, give me no static;
Though Binger may seem to be merely a fictive
Device in this rhyme scheme, his beans were addictive:
Connoisseurs of his verdant, string-straight *Phaseolus*
Claimed that it stood above all others, *solus.*)

The string bean's admirers are ever so many:
There's Artis G. Benn, whose best friends call him Bennie;
There's Gina T. Berns and Brent Gains and Grant Ibsen
(Not an onion, a string bean, for him in his gibson).
When string beans are offered, ah then, reader, then is
The hour of delight for my friends Bart G. Ennis,
Ernst Gabín, Nat S. Bergin, the worthy Art Bensing,
of whom, having sung, by your leave I will then sing
Of dear Gert N. Sabin, G. Bannister (smothers
His burgers in string beans), Ben Gantris and others.
In the land that engendered Siberian huskies
A string bean's a *bauboi* to bean-loving Russkies.
In cafes in Poland, the rule should be "no check"
For diners deprived of their *zielony groszek.*

When *spercieboon*'s mentioned, you're not in Silesia,
But somewhere in Holland, on turf once called Frisia.
Feijão verde's the term that's used in Braganza.
(Bear with me; this litany ends with this stanza.)
And whether he is or he ain't a grammarian,
If your man calls it *zöld bab*, you know he's Hungarian:
The leguminous veggie (to augment these data)
Takes pride of place in his *zöldségsaláta,*
A salad in which there are string beans and mustard
and egg yolks sufficient to make a large custard.
Tua fuk yao is the term throughout all of Thailand,
From Chiang Rai down to Phuket, a southerly island

Where neither our corn or our National Pastime
Are known (no Thai cobs there when I looked the last time).

ENVOI
Keep your samphire, your *mâche*, your ephemeral passions
That flash in the pan like the rag trade's hot fashions;
With no strings attached, *Phaseolus vulgaris*,
The plebian old string bean, remains *sui generis*.

beat about the bush. The expression derives from literal usage in
the fifteenth century, when hunters armed with wooden bats roused
small, sleeping game birds from within bushes and whacked them
dead as they emerged. The proverbial bird in the hand comes from
the same source.

beef. 1. A complaint ("What's your beef?"); to complain. **2.** Physical heft, BRAWN, muscle ("The quarterback was trampled by six
hundred pounds of beef on the hoof"). **3.** (usually with "up") To
reinforce, add impact to ("We've got to beef up the war on war").
4. Any bovine animal raised for meat. Ultimately from the Latin
bōs ("ox").

beer. Middle English *ber(e)*, Old English *bēor*, via West Germanic
from Late Latin *biber*, "a drink," from Latin *bibere*, "to drink." A
brewskie; that in which those hoping for more than is reasonable
expect to find egg.

   beer and skittles. Easeful existence; that which life isn't all.

   beer, small. Weak beer, hence a person or matter of little consequence. "To suffer fooles, and chronicle small Beere," wrote Shakespeare in *Othello*.

beet. An alternative to lobster in similes for redness. According to one published factoid, the word is from the French *bête* ("beast"), supposedly because some Medieval cook saw a resemblance between the cut veggie and a butchered animal. There is zero etymological evidence to support the claim and every reason to laugh it out of court. Although the Middle English *bete* and Old English *bēte* are spelled with the same letters as *bête*, the modern English "beet" is from the Latin *bēta*, with no French connection. "Beast" (Middle English *beste*) *is* from Old French but by an entirely different route, the starting point of which was the Latin *bestia*.

benedict, eggs. Sooner or later, we all have our fifteen minutes of fame, which may account for the obscurity of some food eponyms. According to Sharon Tyler Herbst, the author of *Food Lover's Companion*, the "most popular legend of the dish's origin says that it originated at Manhattan's famous Delmonico's Restaurant [which of the several famous Delmonico's restaurants unspecified] when regular patrons, Mr. and Mrs. LeGrand Benedict, complained that there was nothing new on the lunch menu." In *his* book, *Why You Say It,* Webb Garrison tells us that "legend suggests that Saint Benedict is responsible for the combination of foods that seem to bear his name. Oral tradition long current in greater New York City credits the term to wealthy Samuel Benedict, about whom little is known.

"Many scholars say that neither the saint nor the New Yorker had anything to do with creating and naming the perennially popular dish. [Perennially popular the dish may be, but not millennially; Saint Benedict of Nursia ate his last brunch in A.D. 543, and it takes neither a scholar nor a brain surgeon to discount the notion that he might have been present at the creation or the christening.] Instead, they say, it stems directly from the culinary interests of banker-yachtsman E. C. Benedict."

Having trotted out one absurdity and two possibilities, with nothing to support any of the three but "legend suggests," "oral tradition credits" and "they say," Garrison vaults to the unequivocal conclusion that "we still use the water-loving banker's name to designate the dish."

To toss one more piece of conjecture into the debate, couldn't the eponym in question have been a lower-case benedict—a confirmed bachelor newly wed? Consider: Eggs benedict traditionally are served in couples, bedded together on ham and blanketed in hollandaise. The nuptial couch? Well, perhaps not; the egg's misfortune is that it gets laid only once.

billi bi. As in the case of the preceding entry, the identity of the dedicatee is conjectural. Sharon Tyler Herbst: "Though there are several stories of the [creamed mussel] soup's origin, the most popular is that Maxim's chef Louis Barthe named it after . . . American tin tycoon William B. (Billy B.) Leeds." Here, as above, "most popular" seems to imply "most plausible," while preserving the writer's neutrality. On the same subject, the usually magisterial *Larousse*

Gastronomique is even more circumspect: "Billy by [*sic*] or billibi [is] said to have been created by Barthe, the chef of Maxim's, for a regular customer called Billy, who *adored* mussels [italics added; "adored" seems somewhat overly vivid in the context of hearsay evidence about a guy without a surname]. Other sources claim that billy by was invented in Normandy, after the Normandy landings, when a farewell dinner was given for an American officer called Bill. So it was called 'Billy, bye bye,' which degenerated to 'Billy by.'" But of course.

bird's nest soup. Anyone who denigrates anything as "not worth a bucket of warm spit" hasn't priced the salient ingredient of this classic Chinese soup lately. Many non-Chinese assume that the term is simply a literal translation of some fanciful conceit, like the hyperbolic "thousand-year egg," but they're mistaken in the case of the genuine article. An ersatz, not-very-convincing knockoff of authentic bird's nest soup, made mostly with egg whites and cornstarch, turns up in some inferior restaurants, priced at about what it's worth. The real McCoy, prohibitively expensive, is made from the actual nests of a swiftlike bird, which are constructed mostly of the bird's viscous spittle.

biscuit. The British term for what's more commonly called "cookie" in the United States. The somewhat tentative finding among etymologists is that the word may be from the Medieval Latin *biscoctus* ("twice-cooked"). Potters apply it to unglazed ceramics subjected to a single firing (as they do another culinary term, "bisque"). Shakespeare made a halfhearted attempt to use it imagistically in *As You Like It* ("As drie as the remainder bisket after a voyage"), but it wasn't until the 1940s, when the sportswriter Red Smith described the light-heavyweight boxer Gus Lesnevitch as "biscuit-faced" that the word's potential was fully, startlingly realized.

Borscht Belt. The locus, in the Catskill Mountains of New York state, of a constellation of resort hotels renowned as incubators of comedic and musical talent. So called for the soup of choice among the region's largely Russian-Jewish vacationers.

Boston strawberries. Baked beans.

boysenberry. A hybrid of the LOGANBERRY and various blackberries and raspberries, named for its twentieth-century American developer, Rudolph Boysen.

brawn. 1. (chiefly British) A pig. **2.** A pickled or preserved dish, such as head cheese, made from a pig's head, feet or other spare parts. **3.** Muscle, weight, strength.

brisket. The butcher's term for the ribs and meat from an animal's chest derives in succession from the Middle English *brusket* and, probably, from what the American Heritage Dictionary offers as "a Scandinavian compound akin to Old Norse *brjost*" ("breast").

brunch. The portmanteau ("breakfast" cum "lunch") term first appeared in print in 1900. Originator unknown.

Buffalo chicken wings. So named for their city of origin in New York state, where they were created at the Anchor Bar.

burgoo. A.k.a. "Kentucky burgoo," this thick, meaty stew of the

American South, originally made with small game, takes its name from an oatmeal porridge served to eighteenth-century British seamen. The noun possibly derives via the Arabic from the Persian *burghul* ("crushed grain").

burrito. Mexican Spanish "little donkey," for the stuffed TORTILLA's perceived resemblance to the beast of burden.

butter. The noun is traceable through Middle and Old English, West Germanic and the Latin *butyrum* to the Greek *bouturon* ("cow cheese").

> **butter-and-eggs.** The North American plant *Linaria vulgaris*, which bears a spike of pale-yellow and orange blossoms.

> **butter-and-egg man, big.** A derisive term applied by American GIs of World War II to male civilians, especially those who competed for the attention of women by spending more generously than most servicemen could. Possibly coined by Texas Guinan.

> **butter-and-sugar.** A type of sweet corn bearing yellow and white kernels.

> **butterball.** A chubby person; a bird, usually a turkey, commercially so designated for its plumpness by a major producer.

> **butterfingers.** A klutz.

> **butter up.** To flatter or ingratiate oneself with.

C

cabbage. From Middle English *caboche* and an Old North French variant of the Old French *caboce*, or "head." Hence, such common terms as "cabbagehead" and "head of cabbage" are tautological. Slang for money, especially paper money. See also p. 16.

cabbage butterfly. Any of several butterflies of the genus *Pieris* that feed largely on cabbages. Known in the caterpillar stage as "cabbage worm."

cacciatore. Italian "hunter." Dishes prepared *alla cacciatore* are cooked in the style of hunters, with mushrooms and other foraged foods salient among the ingredients. The precise French equivalent of the term is *chasseur*.

caciocavallo. Literally "horse cheese." A southern Italian cow cheese, supposedly once made from mare's milk.

Caesar salad. See p. 18.

cake, piece of. Any action brought off with minimal difficulty and effort, a snap.

cake, take the. To outdo anything or anyone of a comparable nature: "For bald-faced lies, that one takes the cake."

cakewalk. Originally, a stylized promenade or walk, with cakes awarded for the execution of the most original or intricate steps. Later, a strutting dance derived therefrom. An easy victory in any sort of competition: "The game was a cakewalk for the Beavers."

cambric tea. A hot, pallid beverage of sweetened watered milk, usually laced with a little tea. Named for the thin white fabric it supposedly resembles, which takes *its* name from the French textile manufacturing town of Cambrai.

canapé. From the French for "couch." Any small savory "seated" on bread, toast, a cracker or the like.

canard. French "duck." A defamatory story or rumor without foundation or based on a half-truth. From the expression *vendre des canards à moitié* ("to half-sell ducks").

candy. Ultimately traceable to the Tamil *kantu,* via Arabic *quand* and the *candi* of Old Italian, Old French and Middle English, with a possible Sanskrit antecedent. In limited use, a term of endearment, as in the song lyric "I call my sugar candy."

candy, nose. Cocaine.

candy stripes. A decorative device or motif of alternating, usually red and white, stripes, resembling a traditional form of candy decoration.

canola oil. The promotional euphemism given to rapeseed oil by the Canadian cooking oil industry.

cantaloupe. Named for the papal villa of Cantalupo, outside Rome, where the melon, indigenous to India, was grown in Europe for the first time. In plural, slang for the female breasts.

carpaccio. So named because an exhibition of the eponymous Renaissance painter's works was on view in the city when the dish (of raw sliced beef drizzled with olive oil and lemon juice) was created at Harry's Bar, in Venice. The term has been applied to other foods, such as raw tuna, in recent years by restaurateurs not above taking liberties with established culinary nomenclature.

carrot. Believed by the ancients to strengthen sight—rightly, as it later turned out.

carrot and stick. Originally a device designed to impel horses and mules forward by fastening a stick to the animal's neck and dangling a carrot from it, just beyond grasping distance of the mouth. Figuratively, any reward promised but withheld for unreasonable periods of time or withdrawn altogether, a tantalization. The term gradually has undergone a change of interpretation over the years and now is widely understood to express the alternatives of reward (the carrot) or punishment (the stick).

casaba. From Kasaba (now Turgutlu), Turkey, whence the melon was introduced to the United States in the late nineteenth century.

cashew. The word entered English by way of the Portuguese *cajú* and *acajú*, the latter directly from the Tupi language of aboriginal Brazil.

cassia. See CINNAMON AND CASSIA.

catchup, catsup. See KETCHUP.

cauliflower. From the Italian for "flowered cabbage." According to Mark Twain, "nothing but a cabbage with a college education."

cauliflower ear. Pugilism's badge of honorable ineptitude: an auricle deformed by repeated hooks to the side of the head.

caviar. Figuratively, anything beyond the means or appreciative capacities of ordinary people, as in Shakespeare's "caviar to the general." Literally, the roe of the sturgeon, according to purists, although the term is applied to other types of fish eggs by the less fastidious. See also p. 129.

caviar, eggplant. A somewhat grandiose term for the mashed pulp of baked or broiled eggplant, so called for its small, granular seeds, which bear a vague resemblance to the real McCoy.

cayenne pepper. Both the powdered or flaked condiment (made from the fruit of *Capsicum frutescens*) and Cayenne, the capital of French Guiana, probably trace their names through various orthographic permutations to the Tupi *kyinha.* In the case of the spice, the name gradually is being superseded by the generic "red pepper."

cereal. Curiously, the generic word for the edible-grain-bearing grasses—collectively the largest part of the human diet by far—has given only its literal meaning to the language and has inspired nothing figurative or proverbial. From Ceres, the Roman goddess of agriculture and counterpart of the Greek Demeter.

chayote. A native American mainstay of the Maya and Aztec diets, the squashlike gourd has become a symbol of piety among Buddhists since its importation into Asia, where the pear-shaped fruit's tapering lobes suggest the steepled fingers of the praying Gautama. Although known in West Indian French as *christophine,* the chayote is termed "mirliton" in the French-speaking districts of Louisiana.

cheese. Defined by Clifton Fadiman as "milk's leap toward immortality." See also p. 150.

> **cheese, big.** A Medieval term of envious respect for those who could afford to buy whole wheels of cheese at a time. Hence also "big wheel." Both often used sarcastically today. See also p. 49.

> **cheese-paring.** Miserly in the extreme. The skinflint who saves

and makes such use as can be made of what others would discard as worthless is a cheese parer.

cherry. Supposedly from Cerasus, Turkey, known for the quality of its cherries. In plural form, what life is just a bowl of, according to an old pop song. See also p. 58.

chestnut. 1. A stale joke, hackneyed expression, etc. **2.** The color of red-brown hair. **3.** A horse of the same color. **4.** (plural) What one pulls from the fire when a venture at immediate risk is salvaged.

chicken. 1. To lose one's nerve (usually before "out" or after "turn"). **2.** A game or contest whose object is to force an opponent to give ground or cut and run when at maximum risk, often played with cars on a head-on collision course. Related anatomical adjective forms are "chicken-hearted" and the synonymous "chicken-liv-ered." **3.** A young woman (or, more often, a not-so-young woman, who is said to be "no spring chicken") **4.** A penis (see p. 61). **5.** The cosubject with "egg" of a CHESTNUT concerned with prece-dence. **6.** The subject of an equally venerable CHESTNUT having to do with why said subject traverses a traffic artery.

    chicken colonel. A full colonel in the U.S. Army, recognizable by his "chicken" (i.e., eagle) insignia.

    chicken feed. An insignificant amount, usually of money.

    chicken shit, chickenshit. Irritatingly inessential duties, re-quirements, regulations, etc.; used adjectivally for one who assigns too much chicken shit to a subordinate.

chicory. Nomenclatural confusion abounds here. With regional differences, "chicory" is the name commonly given to the plant *Cichorium intybus*, its edible leaves and its roasted ground root; to the curly endive, *Cichorium endiva*, to the Belgian endive (a.k.a. *witloof*, or "white leaf") and to escarole and radicchio—all fraternal twins but most dissimilar in form, color and, to a lesser extent, flavor. (The taxonomic *intybus* possibly found its way into Latin from the Egyptian *tybi*, or "January," the plant's peak growing month in the lower Mediterranean region.) The aforementioned roasted root, a.k.a. "succory," is used as a coffee substitute or additive, especially in French-speaking regions, notably including Creole Louisiana.

chile, chili, chilli. The word originated as *chilli* in the Nahuatl of the Aztecs, then was Hispanicized as *chile* by the conquistadores and later Americanized as "chili." "Chile" is the preferred spelling today, at least in references to any of the more pungent capsicum peppers, while "chili" usually denotes oils, pastes, powders and sauces made from chiles and dishes of chiles with meat or meat and beans ("chili con carne," a portion of which is "a bowl of red" in Texas). Although the Inca were indigenous to what later coincidentally came to be called Chile, their word for the capsicums was *ají*. In most modern languages, including English, the word "pepper" (in one variation or another) is the term of choice, but it's a misnomer in any of them.

chili, hot. A lubricious woman, especially an ethnic Hispanic in North America.

chipped beef. Creamed and bedded on toast, the stuff is remembered with mixed emotions by veterans of several wars as the "shit on a shingle" served in most mess halls.

chips. The Brit term for what Americans call "fries." American chips are "crisps" in Blighty.

chitterlings. Customarily pronounced *chitlins* in the American South, the small intestines of pigs were chitterlings in Middle English, possibly a diminutive of the Old English *cieter*, "small intestine."

chocolate. See p. 16.

chokecherry. Any of several wild North American cherries suitable for preserves but not for out-of-hand eating. The name derives from their extreme astringency before the addition of sweeteners.

chop. Derived from the Middle English *chappen*, "to split."

chopped liver. A metaphor for insignificance, as in "What am I, chopped liver?" or "Two million bucks ain't just chopped liver." Probably a BORSCHT BELT coinage.

chops. The jaws, cheeks or jowls of an animal. To figuratively lick one's chops is to indicate appetency for or satisfaction with what has been eaten or gleefully to anticipate a killing of some sort.

chow. Food, grub, especially in the American military. Possibly a pidgin rendering of the Mandarin Chinese *ch'ao* ("stir," "fry," "cook").

chow down. 1. Tuck into food, tie on the feedbag. **2.** Perform oral sex.

chow-chow. The word for the mustard-bound mixed vegetable relish, introduced into the United States by nineteenth-century Chinese railroad workers, is probably a pidgin English reduplication of the Mandarin *cha* ("mixed").

chowder. See p. 26.

chutney. From Hindi *catni*. See p. 104.

cinnamon and cassia. Termed "sweet wood" in the Orient, true cinnamon is the dried inner bark of the evergreen tree *Cinnamomum zeylanicum,* a member of the laurel family native to Sri Lanka and India. It and its near-double cassia are two of the world's oldest spices and appear to have been well established as culinary and ritual ingredients long before the Old Testament, with its frequent references to both, was written. Marketed as "cinnamon" (and legally so labeled in the United States), cassia (*C. cassia*) has just about completely supplanted true cinnamon in modern use, but that's nothing new under the sun. In Exodus, the Lord instructs Moses to make an ointment for the consecration of the tabernacle of the congregation of the children of Israel, using (among other ingredients) two hundred fifty shekels of "sweet cinnamon" and twice that amount of cassia; in the second century A.D. Galen maintained that "the finest cassia differs so little from the lowest quality cinnamon that the first may be substituted for the second, provided a double weight of it be used."

Along with pepper, cinnamon was the most sought-after spice of the Classical and later Roman eras. Such was its value that Nero, never one to shun a roaring blaze, is supposed to have vented his grief in the most extravagant possible fashion during his deceased wife's obsequies—by burning enough cinnamon to supply the city of Rome for a year.

The Arabs had locked up the cinnamon trade centuries earlier and had devised elaborate security measures to ensure that their monopoly wouldn't be broken. These included the dissemination of several preposterous myths concerning their sources. One such was swallowed hook, line and sinker by Herodotus, in the fifth century B.C. "Where [cinnamon] comes from and what country produces it, they [the Arabs] do not know," he wrote. "What they say is that the dry sticks, which we have learned from the Phoenicians to call cinnamon, are brought by large birds which carry them to their nests . . . on mountain precipices which no man can climb." In Herodotus's secondhand account, various animals were butchered "into very large joints" below the precipices and left on the ground for the birds to scavenge and schlep back to their aeries. The weight of the meat turned out to be too much for the nests, which tumbled to earth, leaving the canny Arabs to play pick-up-sticks with the cinnamon.

What Herodotus and his contemporaries were taught by the Phoenicians "to call cinnamon" didn't sound much different from what we call cinnamon today, except for a hard initial consonant. The Greeks pronounced the word *kinna(mŏ)mon*, received via the Phoenicians from the Hebrew *qinnåmown*.

Cassia—a.k.a. "false cinnamon," "bastard cinnamon," "Chinese cinnamon" and "canelle"—was rather cavalierly dismissed by a fifteenth-century Englishman, John Russell, in his *Boke of Nurture*. "Synamome," he wrote, was fit "for lordes," but canelle only for "commyn people." The word "cassia," like "cinnamon," has remained virtually unchanged throughout recorded history. The Akkadians called it *kasîa*.

cioppino. See p. 27.

clabber. Eaten or drunk (depending on its consistency) mostly in the British Isles and southern United States, this soured unpasteurized milk previously was called "bonnyclabber," a redundant splicing together of the Irish *bainne* ("milk"), derived from the Middle Irish *banne* ("a drop") and *clabair* ("thick sour milk"). Thus the modern word goes back to Square One, having dropped off some excess baggage along the way.

clam. An old form of "clamp," descriptive of the mollusk's talent for tightening its valves.

clam, happy as a. A shortened form of "happy as a clam in mud," analogous to "happy as a pig in shit." Both expressions assume more than the subjects, especially the clam, are prepared to corroborate.

clam up. Turn off the verbal communication, zip the lip.

clove. See p. 31.

cobbler. All dictionaries consulted were at a loss for words concerning the derivation of the term, as denotative of either the deep-

dish pie or the alcoholic punch. Perhaps the thick-soled pie reminded its christener of shoe leather. Perhaps not.

cockle. A single valve of this bivalve mollusk historically has been
worn as a badge of identity by Catholic pilgrims, especially on the
roads to Santiago de Compostela.

> **cockles of one's heart.** The origin of this expression for one's
> innermost feelings is obscure. Cockles, edible mollusks of the
> family Cardiidae, are generally heart-shaped, though.

coconut. Slang for the human head. Coincidentally, *coco* (Spanish
from Portuguese) translates as "goblin" or "bogeyman," and *hacer
cocos* as "pull faces" or "make eyes." The name is believed to have
been given to the fruit of the palm *Cocos nucifera* because the three
dark spots at the coconut's base resemble a grotesque or grimacing
face.

cole slaw. From the Dutch *kool* ("cabbage") and *sla* ("salad").

collard. Dialect form of "colewort" (genus *Brassica*).

compote. See p. 42.

conch. The Greeks had a word for it, *konkhē,* and most other Western words for it derive therefrom. In standard Italian it's *conchiglia,*
but it's *scungilli* in the dialect of Naples, where the gastropod mollusk of the genus *Strombus* is extensively eaten. In a final remove
from the original form, the *other* nickname of "the Reading Rifle,"
Carl Furillo of the 1955 World Champion Brooklyn Dodgers, was
Skoonj.

consommé. French "concentrate," from Old French *consommer,* "to sum up." Descriptive of the process of boiling a broth down to its essence.

cookie. From *koekje,* the Dutch diminutive for "cake." A term of affection or mild endearment.

> **cookie-cutter.** An adjective for repetitious or rote conformity, as in "a cookie-cutter mentality."
>
> **cookie jar.** What guilty parties are found with their hands in.
>
> **cookies, pop (or toss) one's.** To vomit.

corn, corned. See pp. 54–55.

couscous. see p. 120.

crackling. From the onomatopoeic "crack." In *A Dissertation Upon Roast Pig* by Charles Lamb (or was it *A Dissertation Upon Roast Lamb* by Charles Pig?), the essayist wrote: "There is no flavour comparable, I will contend, to that of the crisp, tawny, well-watched, not over-roasted, *crackling,* as it is well called—the very teeth are invited to their share of the pleasure at this banquet in overcoming the coy, brittle resistance."

cranberry. Originally "craneberry," because the shrub's blossoms were thought to resemble the heads of the cranes that frequent cranberry bogs. Also called "bounceberry" for its resiliency when ripe.

crawfish, crayfish. Also called "crawdad" and "mudbug." In America, the northerner's "cray" sticks in the southerner's "craw."

cream. 1. The richest or most satisfying part, as in "the cream of the crop." **2.** That which proverbially rises to the top. **3.** To flatten or defeat decisively.

cream puff. A softy, a pushover. A term of endearment.

croissant. As it happens, the emblematically French breakfast roll originated in Budapest in 1686, after a Turkish siege of the city was broken. As the story goes, alert bakers heard the Turks tunneling beneath their ovens and spread the alarm. The Turks were repulsed, and the bakers thenceforth were privileged to commemorate their vigilance by producing rolls in the shape of the yellow crescent flown on the Ottoman flag. Later, their French counterparts used a lighter, richer dough to produce a flakier crescent (*croissant*), and a symbol of triumph over the Turks was transformed into a symbol of French gastronomy.

cruller. From the Dutch *krulle* ("curl"), for the deep-fried cake's usually twisted shape.

crumpet. Probably from Middle English *crompid* ("cake").

cucumber. What a cool customer is as cool as.

curry. From Tamil *kari* ("sauce"). The culinary term has nothing to do with the English verb (as used in "curry flavor" or "curry a horse") of altogether different derivation.

custard apple. The cherimoya, a tropical American fruit of the tree *Annona reticulata,* having a custardy pulp.

D

dirty rice. A Louisiana Cajun dish of rice garnished with poultry innards, so called for its discolored appearance.

dolly varden. A colorfully spotted trout, *Salvelinus malma,* named for a nineteenth-century women's costume featuring a flowered skirt and named in turn for a character in Dickens's *Barnaby Rudge,* who wore such a costume.

doughnut, donut. What, according to an old rhyming maxim, one should keep one's eye upon, rather than the hole.

dragon and phoenix. A Cantonese dish of lobster and chicken. See p. 88.

dragon's eye. The longan, *Euphoria longana,* a fruit native to Southeast Asia, whose dark pit and pale pulp resemble an eye.

Drambuie. The brand name of a Scotch whiskey-based liqueur, apparently from the Gaelic *an dram buidheach,* "the dram that satisfies."

drum. Any of various marine and freshwater food fishes of the family Sciaenidae, which emit a deep drumming sound, especially as a mating call.

Du Barry, à la. A characterization for any of several French dishes in which cauliflower is salient. The Countess Du Barry, a favorite of Louis XV, was the dedicatee, but not necessarily because the vegetable was a particular favorite of hers. A tradition of French *haute cuisine* seems to dictate that if any personage's name is associated with a particular ingredient once, it will be invoked for all subsequent treatments of the same ingredient.

duck. Both the noun and the verb (in all its senses) seem to derive from the Old English *ducan*, "to dive," but there's no certainty on the point. **1.** A peculiar or eccentric person, an "odd duck." **2.** To evade or dodge, especially by lowering oneself out of harm's way. **3.** (plural) A British term of affection or endearment.

duck, Bombay. A term coined during the British raj in India for a dish of dried salted fish, usually served with curry sauce.

duck soup. Something easily accomplished, a piece of cake.

dumpling. Origin obscure. Perhaps so called because in some treatments dough is dropped, or *dumped*, into soup or some other hot liquid. **1.** A term of endearment. **2.** A short, chubby individual.

dunk. From Pennsylvania Dutch *dunke*. A basketball shot launched from above the rim, as a doughnut is dunked in coffee.

durian. The large, rankly odoriferous fruit of the Southeast Asian tree *Durio zebethinus*, called "smelly fruit" by English-speaking Asians.

E

eat. Inevitably, the verb for so elemental an activity has been put to myriad figurative uses. The sanitized "chew out," meaning to castigate a subordinate, originated as "eat out [one's] ass." The bitterly anguished or envious eat their hearts out; those who speak before they think are apt to eat their words; and the victims of imprudent transactions eat their losses while others eat high on the HOG. To erode is from the Latin *ērōdere,* "gnaw off" or "eat away." We "eat up" whatever inspires appetency of any sort, including our "eats." "Eat my shorts" and "eat *this*" are expressions of contempt.

eel. The metaphor for slipperiness.

egg. 1. The primal source of life, the earth or the cosmos in many of the world's creation myths. **2.** (plural) What prudence dictates that not all of one's be put in one basket; what an omelet can't be made of without breakage.

> **egg cream.** The soda fountain drink once emblematic of New York City, made with neither egg nor cream.
>
> **egghead.** An intellectual, usually of liberal tendencies. Coined in 1952 for supporters of the unsuccessful presidential candidacy of Adlai E. Stevenson, supposedly with reference to Stevenson's baldness, although his opponent Dwight D. Eisenhower had just as fine a head of skin.
>
> **enchilada.** Mexican Spanish. Seasond with chile.
>
> **enchilada, big.** The most powerful member of a group or organization, the head honcho. Compare "top BANANA" (seldom found in enchiladas), "big CHEESE" (frequently so), and "big FISH" (occasionally).

endive. See CHICORY.

entrecôte. French for "between the ribs," whence the steak is cut.

epicure. After Epicurus, the second-century B.C. philosopher who supposedly advocated the sensual pleasures, notably including eating, as the greatest good.

F

farce. A theatrical piece based on broad improbabilities, a ludicrous or baseless affair. From the Old French *farcir,* "to stuff," as a fowl or other food.

fat. Language is larded with the word in one form or another and various contexts. Examples include Mardi Gras ("Fat Tuesday"), "fat of the land," "a fat contract," "fat city," the biblical "fatted calf," etc. "The fat is in the fire" when a situation is out of control. To "chew the fat" is from old seafaring days, when salt pork was a dietary staple of sailors and tough, fatty pieces of rind were the rations of last resort when more palatable meat ran out. The mastication of these rinds was a time-consuming activity, usually accompanied by long exchanges of complaint, scuttlebutt and the like. The expression eventually found its way ashore and remains part of the living language today.

fava bean. A pleonasm: "fava" is from the Latin *faba,* "bean."

fennel. The word is derived from the Latin *foeniculum,* a variety of fragrant hay. A member of the parsley family, fennel symbolized success in ancient Greece, where it was called *marathon* in commemoration of the site of the famous defeat of the Persians in 490 B.C. In Medieval Europe, fennel was hung over doors to ward off evil spirits and smeared on cow's udders to keep their milk from being soured by witchcraft. In sixteenth-century Italy, the herb was symbolic of flattery, and the American Puritans called it "meeting seed" because the seeds were chewed in church.

fenugreek. From the Latin *fenugraecum,* "Greek hay."

fettucine Alfredo. Created in the 1920s by the Roman restaurateur Alfredo di Lello, who named the dish in his own honor.

fiddlehead fern. This isn't the name of a particular species of edible fern but a generic term for a growth stage of most ferns, edible or not (many aren't), when the upper fronds are still tightly coiled. Also called "ostrich fern."

fig. See p. 58.

filbert. A.k.a. "hazelnut." So named because it ripens on or about Saint Philibert's Day, August 22.

finnan haddie. "Findhorn [a Scottish fishing port] haddock." Salted and smoked haddock, popular as a breakfast dish in Britain.

fish. To seek incriminating evidence or grope one's way to a desired conclusion with no hard evidence in hand. To bring to the surface or general notice, usually with "up," as in "fish up details."

fish, big. Someone of importance, often in a small pond.

fish, cold. One lacking warmth or gregariousness.

fish, dead. What a limp, cold handshake is like. Figuratively, a human corpse.

fish eye. A suspicious glance or stare.

fishnet. An open, revealing weave, as in women's stockings.

fish story. A tall tale.

fishy. Suspect, not quite kosher.

A "fine kettle of fish," usually denoting a less-than-successful enterprise of some sort, derives from an eighteenth-century custom initiated by the landed gentry along the river Tweed—a sort of come-one-come-all fish stew. Occasionally, these parties went awry, prompting the ironic designation for a fiasco of any kind. Eventually, "a different kettle of fish" came to denote any sort of alternative to an expected outcome.

flambé. French "flaming," which is to say, ignited after being doused with a flammable liquor, usually brandy. "Flambéed" is a dumb Americanism that would translate literally as "flaminged."

flauta. Spanish "flute." So termed in Mexican cookery for its shape. A corn TORTILLA, tightly rolled around a savory filling and fried.

flummery. From the Welsh *llymru*. Any of several, chiefly British, soft, bland dishes or puddings, often with an oatmeal base. Figuratively, meaningless flattery, nonsense, blather.

food. From the Old English *foda* ("sustenance") via Middle English *fode*. Metaphorically, that which sustains or nourishes the spirit, emotions ("If music be the food of love, play on"), intellect ("food for thought"), etc. In one of the better gastronomic puns (here's another: "What a friend we have in cheeses"), some anonymous wag twisted Shakespeare's "What fools these mortals be" into "What foods these morsels be."

food, brain. Fish.

food, soul. A term that gained currency in the 1960s, denoting the comestibles popular among African Americans and flaunted, like "Black is beautiful," as an expression of ethnic pride.

foodie. Any member of the professions concerned with the dissemination of culinary and gastronomic information, restaurant personnel and other food service workers usually not included. The term is a spinoff from "groupie" and, although used by its designees, carries some connotations of dilettantism.

fool. An English dessert of puréed fruit (originally gooseberries) and whipped cream. If there is any connection between the cookery term and a clown or nitwit, it may be through the "goose" of "gooseberry" and its synonym as applied to humans.

formaggio. See p. 41.

French fries. There's no solid evidence that these potatoes originated in France (Belgium is at least as likely a candidate), and they are not so termed by the French. In all likelihood, the dish originally was termed "frenched fries," meaning cut into thin strips. In France they're simply *pommes frites* ("fried potatoes"), with no proprietary claims advanced.

fruit. See p. 59.

fruitcake. What a human fruitcake is as nutty as.

fudge. 1. Nonsense, horsefeathers. **2.** An interjection used to express disbelief, irritation, disappointment (usually with "oh"). **3.** To fake or gloss over. **4.** In printing, a piece of filler copy inserted at the end of a short column of type. All probably from *fadge,* an archaic word of uncertain meaning and origin.

fusilli. A spiral-shaped pasta so named for its resemblance to the interior rifling of a gun barrel.

G

garlic. Dracula's nemesis. In sixteenth-century England, "pilgarlic" (i.e., "peeled garlic") was a derisive appellation for a bald head.

geoduck. According to the American Heritage Dictionary, the name of this outsized Pacific Northwest clam (*Panope generosa*) derives from "Chinook jargon *go-duck,*" for whatever *that's* worth. The favored pronunciation is *gooey duck,* which sounds more like *canard a l'orange* than a bivalve mollusk.

gherkin. See p. 59.

ginger. The rhizome of the southern Asian plant *Zingiber officinale,* used as a spice and condiment. From the Sanskrit *singabera* ("horn-shaped," for its resemblance to a deer's antlers). The noun is synonymous with "liveliness," "pep" and the like.

ginseng. From Mandarin Chinese for "man root," for its resemblance to the human figure.

goober. A peanut, from the Angolese *nguba.* A southern American rustic or redneck.

goose. 1. The anserine female for whose mate the same sauce is appropriate. **2.** A silly or flighty individual. **3.** To poke between the buttocks. **4.** To provide fresh impetus to, as in "goose the motor."

> **goose barnacle** or **barnacle goose. 1.** Any of various marine crustaceans of the order Cirripedia, so termed from a Medieval belief that geese were hatched from the creatures, overwhelming empirical evidence to the contrary notwithstanding. One species bears a striking resemblance to a goose's head and neck and is a dangerously harvested, costly delicacy in Spain, where it's termed *percebe.* **2.** Barnacle goose. A waterfowl, *Branta leucopsis,* of northern Europe and Greenland.

goose egg. See pp. 45, 65.

goosefish. See ANGLER FISH.

gooseflesh. Horripilation; bristling of the body hair, as from cold or fear, accompanied by a momentary pimpling of the surrounding skin. Also "goose bumps."

goose hangs high, the. The moment is propitious for merriment or high jinks of one sort or another. Probably from the early nineteenth-century sport of gander-pulling, in which a goose with a greased neck was hung from a tree or pole while riders galloped by, trying to pull the bird's head off. Hey, guys, play nice.

goulash. An Anglicization of the Hungarian *gulyas* ("herdsman's meat"). An undifferentiated mess, as in "made a goulash of it."

gourmet. Anagrammatically, "more gut."

Graham cracker, Graham flour. Whole-wheat products named for Sylvester Graham, a nineteenth-century American vegetarian and dietary reformer.

grape. 1. Originally, a hook with which grapes were harvested and a bunch of grapes collectively. Germanic, akin to "grapnel." The contemporaneous term for a single grape is unknown. **2.** Wine generically, as in "a fondness for the grape." **3.** Grapeshot, a cluster of small balls with which cannon once were loaded.

gravy. An unexpected or unearned dividend.

   gravy train. A job or assignment that yields maximum profit or benefit for minimum effort.

grouper. From the Portuguese *garoupa,* probably from a native South American name.

grouse. See p. 43.

gruel. A thin, watery porridge. To harrow or exhaust, as in "grueling punishment."

guacamole. Mexican Spanish from Nahuatl *ahuacamolli,* "avocado sauce."

H

halibut. See p. 24.

ham. See p. 65.

Hangtown fry. A dish of fried breaded oysters, bacon and scrambled eggs, named for the California gold-rush town where it supposedly originated. Hangtown, so named for its frequent necktie parties, is now Placerville.

hero sandwich. So named for its heroic size and the heroic appetite required for its consumption. Alternative regional terms include "grinder" (possibly from the ground meatballs that are components of some versions), "hoagie" (your guess is as good as any), "submarine" (for its shape), "poor boy" (or "po' boy") and "mufeleta," the last two used around New Orleans.

herring, red. Literally, a smoked herring of reddish color. Figuratively, anything used deliberately to divert attention from the matter at hand. From the use by poachers of red herrings to throw hunting dogs off the scent of their quarry.

hibachi. Japanese "fire bowl."

hoecake. See p. 30.

hog. Aside from the obvious: a Harley-Davidson in motorcyclists' parlance; in rural Britain, a young sheep before its second shearing; in American football, a member of the defensive line. Middle English *hogge* from Old English *hogg*.

hog, high on (or **off**) **the, to live** (or **eat**). To enjoy the best of whatever's available, usually but not necessarily with reference to material rewards. From a widespread preference for meat from the animal's upper legs or body.

hog, whole. Without restraint or inhibition; the whole nine yards. Usually with "go the." According to Charles Earle Funk, it's "highly probable" that the expression arose in early nineteenth-century America and derives from a scurrilous poem, *The Love of the World Reproved; or Hypocrisy Detected,* by William Cowper, which contains the lines, "Thus, conscience freed from every clog/ Mahometans eat up the hog." Funk also speculated that the expression may derive from the English shilling or U.S. dime, each termed a "hog." As his backup theory goes, big spenders "went the whole hog."

hominy. Dried corn kernels, called "samp" in coarser, and "grits" in finer, grinds. From the Algonquian *rockahominy.*

hoppin John. Derivation unknown. Black-eyed peas and rice cooked with salt pork. A southern American dish of probable slave origin, traditionally eaten on New Year's Day to ensure prosperity during the next twelve months. The legumes symbolize coins, and the collards that usually accompany them stand for folding money.

hors d'oeuvre. French (singular and plural) "outside the work," i.e., not included in the preparation of the meal proper.

hotchpotch. See p. 26.

hot dog. The term was coined in 1906, when a popular cartoonist of the day, T.A. Dorgan (Tad) depicted the then newly popular sandwich as a sweaty dachshund on a split bun. Curiously, the Viennese traditionally have termed the sausage *Frankfurter,* while the burghers of Frankfort am Main, placing credit or blame where *they* deem it due, call the same sausage *Wienerwurst.* **1.** A show-boating athlete (see p. 66). **2.** (plural) Overheated feet. **3.** An interjection of delight, enthusiasm, etc., as in "We're having hot dogs? Hot dog!"

hush puppy. See p. 29.

I

Indian nut. The pine nut, piñon, pignola.

Irish potato. See p. 13.

J

jam. Probably from the verb meaning to squeeze tightly.

jambalaya. Louisiana Creole. Probably in part from the French *jambon* ("ham"), a salient ingredient in most versions of the rice-based dish, which derives in part from the *paella* of Spain.

Japanese medlar, Japanese plum. The loquat.

Jerusalem artichoke. See p. 9.

John Dory. See p. 21.

julienne. See p. 37.

junket. A trip or excursion, especially when underwritten by a government agency or some other sponsor. Probably from the ease and sweetness with which the dessert of the same name goes down.

junk food. The term, which needs no definition here, has spawned various spinoffs, such as "junk bonds," "junk food music," "junk food journalism," etc. The operative word is from the Middle English *jonket,* probably of Dutch derivation. Its earliest association with food goes back to the second half of the seventeenth century, when the salted meats or fish eaten at sea were termed "junk" or "saltjunk."

K

ketchup (also catchup, catsup). From Malay *kechap* via Chinese (Amoy dialect) *kōetsiap* or *kētsiap,* combining *kōe* ("minced seafood") and *tsiap* ("sauce"). Actually, Worcestershire sauce is much closer to the original *kechap* than is the tomato-based glop that goes by the name today.

kidney. Disposition, temperament.

kipper, kippered herring. See p. 52.

kitchen. From Middle English *kichine* and *kuchene,* ultimately from Latin *coquere* ("to cook"). In baseball parlance, a pitch that the batter can handle most effectively is "right in his kitchen." The place that Harry Truman advised getting out of "if you can't stand the heat."

kitchen cabinet. An informal group of advisers, usually to a head of state, who hold no official posts.

kitchen midden. A refuse heap from an early culture, made up mostly of culinary detritus and of archaeological interest.

kitchen police, KP. Military enlisted personnel temporarily assigned kitchen duties. Such duties: "I'm on KP today."

kitty mitchell. The speckled hind, a member of the grouper family supposedly named for a Florida prostitute who favored polka-dot dresses when not performing in the buff.

kiwi fruit. A.k.a. "Chinese gooseberry." Named for the hairy flightless bird of New Zealand (the principal producer and exporter) to which the fruit *Actinidia deliciosa* bears a superficial physical resemblance.

knackwurst, knockwurst. German *knack* ("to crack") and *Wurst* ("sausage"), the first syllable being an onomatopoeic rendering of the sound made when the sausage is bitten.

kosher. From the Hebrew *kasher* ("proper," "pure"). Descriptive of foods that conform to Jewish rabbinical laws governing sanitation, ritual purity and various taboos. Figuratively, legitimate, on the up-and-up, usually used negatively, as in "That doesn't seem quite kosher."

kreplach. In Jewish cookery, a filled noodle dumpling. Until a couple of decades ago, the term often was used in New York Chinese restaurants by smart-ass waiters who described wonton as "Chinese kreplach" for the edification of a largely Jewish clientele.

kumquat. Chinese "golden orange."

L

lacrimi cristi. "Tear of Christ," a white wine grown on the slopes of Mount Vesuvius. According to Campanian legend, when Lucifer fell from heaven, the impact on earth created the Bay of Naples. Saddened by the devil's presence in so beautiful a region, Christ shed a tear over Vesuvius, whereupon a grapevine sprouted where it had fallen.

Lady Baltimore cake. A then nameless cake supposedly served to the author Owen Wister and later described in his novel *Lady Baltimore*.

ladyfinger. So called for its putative resemblance to the digit it commemorates. The lady in question may have been an ancestor of Minnie Mouse.

lager. The aged beer takes its name from a German verb meaning "to store."

lamb. A sweet-tempered, gentle being. Jesus Christ, "the Lamb of God." A member of a Christian flock. An easy mark or dupe, one readily fleeced. A term of endearment.

  lamb chop. 1. A term of endearment. **2.** That which, according to the sportswriter Red Smith, the pitcher Lefty Grove could have thrown past a wolf.

lamb's lettuce. Corn salad, *mâche.*

lamprey. Any of various elongated freshwater or anadromous fishes of the family Petromyzontidae. A piscatorial Dracula, this primitive critter is equipped with a jawless mouth with which it sucks up to other fishes in order to feed on their blood. Although not very digestible, the lamprey was much favored in Medieval and early Renaissance England, where Henry I died of "a surfeit of lampreys." As a token of its loyalty to the crown, the city of Gloucester still presents the reigning monarch with a lamprey pie, a local specialty, at Christmas. Also formerly called "lamper eel," although not a true eel.

laurel. See p. 118.

leek. From the Old English *leac* ("spear"). According to E. S. Dallas, "This was at one time so much cultivated in England that the very name for a garden was *leac-tun,* and the very name for a gardener was *leac-ward."* Heavily cultivated though it may have been in England, the leek is the national emblem of Wales.

legume. Although the English word is directly from the French (from the Latin *lūgumen,* "bean"), the French use it more inclusively. Botanically, a legume is a pod that splits in two along its vertical seams, leaving the seeds attached to the lower valve or shell. Look under *legumes* on a French menu, though, and you'll find veggies of all sorts, leguminous or not.

lemon. The symbol and expression for anything that fails to live up to expectations; a dud, particularly a defective car. See also p. 109.

lemons. What sour-faced people look as though they've been sucking.

lentil. The "mess of pottage" that the biblical Esau sold his birthright for was a thick lentil soup, a *potage de lentilles* or *potage Esahu,* as French menu terminology would put it. The legume *Lens esculenta* ("edible lens" for the lenslike shape of the seed) was eaten in the Near East, where it grew wild, in prehistoric times and has been cultivated at least since the Sumerians developed a settled civilization. Like the black-eyed pea of the American South, the lentil is eaten in many parts of the Old World at the onset of the New Year, as an augury of prosperity to come.

lettuce. See p. 17.

lichee, lichi. See LITCHI.

licorice stick. The clarinet.

lima bean. From Lima, Peru, where the conquistadores found it around 1500.

limpet. The edible (but not extensively eaten) mollusks of the families Acemeidae and Patellidae, which characteristically cling tightly to rocks and have given their common name to anyone who clings persistently to another and to an explosive device designed to cling to ships' hulls until detonated. The word derives ultimately from the Medieval Latin *lamprēda* ("lamprey," another clinger). Both one of its family names and its French popular name, *patelle,* are ety-mologically related to the anatomical "patella," or "kneecap," which the limpet's shape resembles.

linguine. Italian "little tongues."

litchi, also **lichee, lichi, lychee.** The fleshy fruit of the Chinese tree *Litchi chimensis,* often inaccurately termed "litchi nut."

littleneck clam. From Little Neck Bay, Long Island, New York, once an important source of the hard-shelled clam, or quahog, *Venus mercenaria.* The term now is used to designate size, littlenecks being the smallest of three grades, including the medium-size cherrystone and appreciably larger chowder clam. The taxonomic *mercenaria,* incidentally, is from the Latin *mercēs* ("pay"), from which the English "mercenary" derives. The quahog's shell was the material of choice for the manufacture of wampum, the monetary unit used in many aboriginal American societies. "Quahog" is from the Narragansett *poquauhock.*

lobster. The alternative to "beet" in similes concerned with redness. The word is rooted in the Latin *locusta* ("locust"), from the crustacean's perceived resemblance to the grasshopper.

lobster Newburg. See p. 18.

lobster shift. A newspaper worker's late-evening or early-morning tour of duty, or the skeleton staff in residence between editions. Also "lobster trick." Origin unknown.

lobster Thermidor. According to one theory, the dish was named by Napoleon, when he tasted it for the first time during the eleventh month (Thermidor) of the French revolutionary calendar. More convincingly, the dish and its name are said to have originated at the Paris restaurant Maire's in January 1894, on the evening of the opening of Victorien Sardou's play *Thermidor.* The same playwright, incidentally, also was the eponym for eggs Sardou, a specialty of the New Orleans restaurant Antoine's.

loganberry. Developed or discovered (botanists disagree about whether it's a hybrid or a distinct species) by J. H. Logan in the late nineteenth century.

loin. See SIRLOIN.

long bean. See under BEAN.

lotus. 1. An aquatic plant, *Nelumbo nucifera,* native to southern Asia, with edible leaves, seeds and roots (rhizomes). **2.** A small tree or shrub, *Zizyphus lotus,* of the Mediterranean region, or its fruit.

>   **lotus eater.** One of a North African people described in the *Odyssey* as living in semidrugged indolence induced by eating the fruit of *Z. lotus.* By extension, any indolent sybarite.

>   **lotus land.** A somewhat snide appellation for southern California and its perceived sybaritic way of life.

love apple. See p. 16.

lunch, free. That which there is no. See also p. 57.

Lyonnaise, à la. If onions don't agree with you, skip any dish so described.

M

macadamia, macadamia nut. The edible seed of the tree *Macadamia ternifolia,* native to Australia but now widely cultivated elsewhere, especially in Hawaii. Named for John L. McAdam, a Scottish-born chemist who initiated its cultivation as a source of food. (The tree previously had been grown exclusively as an ornamental.)

macaroni. Forget any stories you may have heard about an early Italian royal exclaiming *"Ma caroni!"* (roughly, "My dear!") upon first tasting the pasta, which is *maccheroni* in Italian, from the earlier *maccaroni.* Forget, too, about all those Marco Polo legends having to do with how the stuff was brought from Cathay to Italy. The term originally meant "fine paste" and was in use before Marco explored the Orient. See also p. 42.

macaroon. The cookie, made with a fine almond paste, takes its name from the same source as MACARONI.

macedoine. The colorful mélange of cut fruits or vegetables takes its name from "Macedonian," because the population of Macedonia is itself a mélange, ethnically speaking.

macerate. From the Latin *mācerare,* "to soften."

madeleine. Specific foods and dishes have had a pervasive, shaping influence on language in general, but this small French "seashell cake so strictly pleated outside and so sensual inside" has inspired more sustained verbiage than any other comestible in history—all of it written by Marcel Proust. As A. J. Liebling put it, "The Proust *madeleine* phenomenon is now as firmly established in folklore as Newton's apple or Watt's steam engine. The man ate a tea biscuit, the taste evoked memories, he wrote a book. . . . In the light of what Proust wrote with so mild a stimulus, it is the world's loss that he did not have a heartier appetite. On a dozen Gardiner's Island oysters, a bowl of clam chowder, a peck of steamers, some bay scallops, three sautéed soft-shelled crabs, a few ears of fresh-picked corn, a thin swordfish steak of generous area, a pair of lobsters, and a Long Island duck, he might have written a masterpiece." (Liebling's menu specifications would be hard to fill: Clamming is prohibited in Gardiner's Island waters, and the bay scallop season doesn't coincide with those of soft-shelled crabs or fresh-picked corn.)

Thanks to Proust and his *À la recherché de temps perdu,* the word "memories" itself for years has evoked the word "madeleine" for literate people the world over.

maize. See p. 12.

margarine. From the French *margarique,* derived from the Greek *margaron* ("pearl"), for the butter substitute's opalescence in its uncolored form.

marinate. To drink to excess, as in "He marinated himself in juniper consommés."

marinara. See p. 13.

marjoram. Often confused with or substituted for oregano, it was described by Shakespeare as "the herb of grace." The early Greeks wove it into funeral wreaths and planted it on graves, as prayers for the happiness of the deceased in a future life.

marmalade. Portuguese "quince jam," but made mostly from Seville oranges today. One utterly specious legend has it that Mary, Queen of Scots, could be consoled only by the citrus preserve in her frequent, understandable bouts of depression, and that her condition found its way into French as *Marie malade* ("sick Mary"), from which the English word supposedly derives. The root word, however, is almost certainly the Greek *melimēlon* ("honey apple").

marrow. Thoreau wished "to live deep and suck out all the marrow of life." These days, less dedicated suckers eat the soft, fatty tissue on toast or dig it from the interior of bones with a long, slender spoon especially designed for the purpose. Although rarely so used nowadays, "marrow" used to be synonymous with "strength," "vigor" and "vitality." Used figuratively in the expression "chilled to the marrow."

marshmallow. "Marsh mallow" in an earlier day, when the root of the plant *Althea officinalis* provided an extract used in confectionary. The marshmallows some of us toast over open fires today, or use as a garnish in Jell-O salads, are made from corn syrup, gum arabic, synthetic flavorings and gelatine, all but the last unknown to speakers of Middle English, who borrowed their *mershmalwe* from the Old English *meremealwe*.

matelote. See p. 26.

matzoh. The name of the unleavened bread eaten by Jews at Passover is an etymological cousin of "massage." The words' mutual root is the Arabic *massa,* "to touch" or "handle," as in the kneading of dough.

mayonnaise. At least four theories of word origin contend here. According to one, the sauce was named for Port Mahon, on the island of Minorca, after its capture by the Duke of Richelieu in 1756. Another posits Bayonne, France, as the point of origin and "bayonnaise" as the original term. The greatest of all French chefs, Antonin Careme, claimed that the noun derived from the verb *manier* ("to stir") and called his version of the sauce *magnonaise* or *magnionaise.* Finally, Prosper Montagné, the guiding spirit behind the first edition of *Larousse Gastronomique,* advocated *moyeunaise,* derived from *moyeau* ("egg yolk"). Until the debate has been resolved, hold the mayo, maho, bayo, magno, or whatever.

mesclun. A salad of mixed young wild and cultivated shoots, leaves and, sometimes, blossoms. From the Niçois *mesclumo,* "mixture."

milk. 1. The standard comparative (along with "snow") in similes having to do with whiteness. **2.** To draw out or extract, as if by literally milking a dairy animal; To extract information, money, laughter, sympathy, etc., by diligent or prolonged effort ("to milk the audience for laughs"); to draw funds from a "cash cow." **4.** To exploit questionably, illicitly or without compunction, as in "milk the taxpayers." **5.** Any of numerous liquids and solutions having a milky appearance or consistency, as "coconut milk." **6.** A cloudy impurity found in some diamonds. **7.** Metaphorical mildness, as in "the milk of human kindness."

On earth ("milkweed," "milkwort," etc.) as it is in heaven ("the Milky Way"), the primal mammalian aliment traditionally has been among the most prevalent food-related metaphors in most languages, except, as in China, where dairy products play little or no role past infancy.

milk and water. Insipid, feeble, wishy-washy.

milk fever. 1. A mild fever, usually occurring with the onset of lactation. **2.** A disease affecting dairy animals, especially after giving birth.

milkfish. A large food fish, *Chanos chanos,* of the Pacific and Indian oceans, so called for its milky color.

milk glass. An opaque or translucent white glass.

milk leg. See p. 63.

milk-liverered. Cowardly, gutless.

milk, mother's. Figuratively, anything that sustains or nourishes the body or spirit. Used facetiously by hard drinkers to describe their booze of choice.

milk run. A relatively risk-free military aerial mission, an easy routine errand.

milk sickness. A.k.a. "trembles." An acute affliction caused by ingesting the milk or milk-derived foods from cattle infected by eating white snakeroot.

milksop. A male lacking manliness, a sissy.

milk tooth. A temporary first tooth or "baby tooth."

milk vetch. Any of various plants of the genus *Astragalus,* believed to increase milk production in goats.

milkweed. Any of various plants, especially of the genus *Astragalus* (see preceding) that exude a milklike juice.

mille-feuilles. French "thousand leaves." A pastry, similar to a Napoleon, made up of alternating layers of puff pastry and sweet filling.

millet. 1. A cereal grass, *Panicum miliacum,* cultivated in Eurasia and North Africa for its grain and in North America as pasture grass and for hay. According to one sixteenth-century writer, the word is from the Latin "millium . . . having as it were a thousand grains in an ear," but the finding is etymologically dubious. **2.** A disease of the mouth, especially in infants.

mince. 1. To cut or chop food into very small pieces. **2.** Food so cut or chopped. **3.** To speak in an affected way ("mince words"), giving more attention to details than the sense of the whole utterance. ("I know no way to mince it in love," says Shakespeare's Henry V, "but directly to say 'I love you.' ") **4.** To walk with very small steps, as though cutting a normal stride into unnaturally small segments. Via Late Latin *minūtia* from Latin *minuere,* "to diminish."

mincemeat. The precursor of ground forcemeat, prepared by mincing meat. A spiced mixture of minced fruits, nuts and suet, spiked with brandy or rum and allowed to mature before use in a cake, pudding or pie. Figuratively, what one is reduced to by a severe beating or tongue-lashing.

minestrone. Italian "big soup" from *minestra* ("soup"). *Minestrina* is a "small soup" or thin broth.

mint. Named for Minthes, a nymph of classical mythology turned into a mint plant by Proserpine, the jealous wife of Pluto. The word is unrelated to the monetary mint.

mirepoix. A mixture of chopped vegetables sautéed in fat and used to season sauces, soups and stews. French co-opted into English for want of anything better. Here's E. S. Dallas on the subject:

> *It is probable that one of these days the common sense of mankind will rise in rebellion against this word and abolish it. What is the Duke of Mirepoix to us because his wife was amiable to Louis XV?*
>
> If she be not fair to me,
> What care I how fair she be?
>
> *The Duke of Mirepoix made himself convenient to the king, and his name is now convenient to the people—the convenient name for the faggot of vegetables that flavours a stew or sauce.*

molasses. The thick sugar syrup, especially in January, that the slowest are as slow as.

monkfish. See ANGLER FISH.

moonshine. Illegally distilled corn whiskey, so named because it usually was cooked by night, when smoking stills were less likely to be detected by the authorities. Foolishness, idle flattery, usually of a romantic nature. There may or may not be a connection between both meanings of the term.

mother. English truncation from the French *mère de vinaigre* ("mother of vinegar," a slimy bacterial glob used as a fermentation agent for converting wine or cider to vinegar).

mountain (or Rocky Mountain) oyster. Usually plural, as are the animal testicles which the term euphemizes. Also called "prairie oysters."

mousse. French "froth," whether it's put in the mouth or on the hair.

muffin. Probably from Low German *Muffen,* plural of *Muffe* ("cake").

Mulligan stew. A catchall ragout widely eaten in turn-of-the-century hobo camps. Probably a specialty of the eponymous, otherwise unidentified cook.

mulligatawny. British raj rendering of the Tamil *milagutanni(r),* "pepper water."

mushroom. To proliferate suddenly, as mushrooms do after rain.

mushroom cloud. The aerial phenomenon produced by an atomic explosion, especially as seen above Hiroshima on August 6, 1945. For its shape and rapid growth.

mussel. See p. 27.

must. Unfermented or incompletely fermented grape juice during the winemaking process. Ultimately from the Latin *mustum,* "new wine."

mustard. A spice or paste made from the seed of any of numerous plants of the family Cruciferae. Ultimately from the Latin *mustum ardens* ("hot must"), so termed because the paste originally was made by mixing the seed with MUST. In a wordless exchange of messages in 334 B.C., Darius III of Persia is supposed to have sent Alexander the Great a large bag of sesame seed, symbolic of the vast number of troops under his command. Alexander's reply: a bag of mustard seed, to signify not only the number of *his* men but their strength.

The mustard seed is one of the smallest known but produces one of the largest of the annual herbaceous plants, a phenomenon recorded in Matthew 13:31–32:

> *Another parable put he forth unto them, saying, The king-dom of heaven is like to a grain of mustard seed, which a man took, and sowed in his field: which indeed is the least of all seeds: but when it is grown, it is the greatest among herbs, and becometh a tree.*

Mustard paste was formed into dense balls for retail sale in Elizabethan England, and the town of Tewkesbury was known widely enough as a leading commercial producer to enable Shakespeare to expect to be understood by the groundlings when they heard "His wit's as thick as Tewkesbury mustard" during the performance of *Henry IV, Part II.* To Anatole France, "a tale without love is like beef without mustard: an insipid dish." And to Pope John XXII, mustard was important enough to merit creation of a special Vatican post (filled by His Holiness's nephew), *grand moutardier du pape.* More currently, "the mustard" is that which the losers among us can't cut and the heat put on a pitcher's fastball.

mustard gas. A chemical warfare weapon, so called for its acrid mustardlike odor.

mustard plaster. An alternative to LIMPET as a symbol of adhesiveness, as in "stuck to her like a mustard plaster."

mutton. From Old French *mouton* ("sheep") via Middle English *moto(u)n.*

muttonchops. Side whiskers shaped as described by their name.

muttonchop sleeves. A style in which the sleeves of a woman's dress or blouse are tightly fitted from the wrist to about the middle of the upper arm, where they take on a balloonlike configuration.

muttonfish. See ABALONE.

N

navel orange. Named for the resemblance of the fruit's blossom base to a belly button.

navy bean. So named for its use as a staple of U.S. Navy messes since the mid-nineteenth century.

noodle. The head; what one is advised to use when cogitation is required. To improvise music, ideas, etc., casually or tentatively. From the German *Nudel.*

   noodle, limp (or wet). Used in similes for flaccidity.

Nova, Novy. Smoked Nova Scotia salmon, especially in the patois of New York deli society.

nut. 1. A more or less crazy person. The precise meaning and many nuances vary, depending on circumstances, intonation and body language, but a nut can range from the party goof who wears a lampshade as a hat to the screwball whose deportment is always somewhat out of synch with generally accepted norms; from a harmlessly bizarre eccentric to a homicidal maniac harboring delusional grievances (usually with "case"). **2.** A difficult, stubborn person or problem, "a hard nut to crack." **3.** Cash invested up front or subsequently expended before any return is realized, as in "a large nut to carry." **4.** Regularly paid operating or living expenses. **5.** The pith, essence or meat of an idea, argument, parable, etc. **6.** A testicle. **7.** The human head. **8.** A bolt's female mate.

nuts. Crazy.

nuts, soup to. The entire gamut, the works, the whole ball of wax.

nutshell. The metaphor invariably invoked for concision.

O

oakleaf. A variety of lettuce, for the shape of its leaves.

oats, feel one's. To act in a frisky or exuberant manner, originally said of horses.

oats, know one's. To be savvy about or familiar with a subject, as horses supposedly are about their food.

oats, sow one's wild. The expression has been in use at least since the sixteenth century, when one English writer characterized late youth and early manhood as "that wilful and unruly age, which lacketh ripeness and discretion, and (as wee say) hath not sowed all their wyeld Oates." The wyeld Oates in question are a cereal grass (*Avena fatua*) that marginally has escaped weedhood, is of little value as a food and is difficult to eradicate from wherever it takes root. Young men were believed to live a life of folly comparable to the folly of sowing wild oats.

octopus. A powerful, far-reaching organization or conglomerate. A guy with roving hands.

offal. Middle English from Middle Dutch *avfal* ("that which falls off"). Offal, a.k.a. "innards" or "organ meats," have managed to get themselves such a bum rap linguistically that they now are assigned such euphemisms as "variety meats" or, in France, "the fifth quarter." The problem is that the word also has denoted refuse since it entered the language. "Garbage," a contemporaneous term, was precisely synonymous in both definitions in its original usages, with no pejorative connotations in culinary usage; a cookbook of 1430 instructs its readers in the preparation of "fayre garbagys of chyckonys." Although "offal" survives marginally today as a designation for such delicacies as goose liver, veal sweetbreads and calf's brain, the culinary "garbage" has been relegated irrevocably to the garbage pail.

olive. The Old World evergreen tree *Olea europaea* is one of the world's earliest cultivated plants, preceded only by some cereal grains and perhaps the date palm. (Olive trees planted in the time of Jesus still bear fruit.) It's believed to have been introduced into Egypt in wild form by Asiatic nomads in the eighteenth century B.C., but when cultivation began is uncertain. Oil was being pressed from its fruit at least as early as 3000 B.C. The tree, its branches and its fruit respectively symbolize longevity, peace and fruitfulness in general.

> **olive oil.** In Italy, the finest oil from the first pressing of the fruit is classified "extra virgin"—a term that makes the same sort of literal sense as "slightly pregnant."

olla podrida. In what may seem to be a misguided stab at truth-in-advertising, the Spaniards named one of their great national dishes—a meal-in-a-pot comprising several courses served successively—"putrid stew."

omelet. What proverbially can't be made without egg breakage.

onion. Often invoked metaphorically in conjunction with conceptualization having many layers of meaning, or with entities greater than the sum of their parts. Also used metaphorically to indicate knowledge of a subject, as in "She knows her onions."

> **Onions.** In a book on food and language, mention must be made of Charles Talbut Onions (1873–1965), an editor of the OED and author of the *Oxford Dictionary of English Etymology*—a man who knew his name about words.

> **onionskin.** A thin, translucent paper, so named for obvious reasons.

orange(s). What apples proverbially shouldn't be compared with. See also p. 43.

oregano. From the Greek "joy of the mountain."

osso buco. The term, which combines the Italian nouns meaning "bone" and "hole," seems to imply slim pickings to anyone who is unfamiliar with this sumptuous treatment of braised veal shank (which is quite meaty in its better versions). To the initiate, though, it's the bone that yields up the dish's crowning glory: its marrow.

oven. What a pregnant woman has a bun in.

oyster. 1. What the world is to anyone who's got it on a string. **2.**

A small muscle found in the pelvic bone of fowl and considered a delicacy. **3.** Any special delicacy. **4.** Any special benefit. **5.** A taciturn person.

oystercatcher. Any of several shore birds of the genus *Haematopus.*

oyster crab. A diminutive crab, *Pinnotheres ostream,* that lives as a roommate of sorts inside a live oyster's shell. Eaten whole and considered a rare delicacy by connoisseurs.

oyster plant. A.k.a. "vegetable oyster." Salsify, the root of the plant *Trapogon portiflius,* from its color when peeled and flavor when cooked.

P

paella. Catalan for "frying pan," via Old French and Latin from the Greek *patanè* ("dish").

pain perdu. French "lost bread." "French toast" in English.

pancake. The inescapable metaphor for flatness. A type of cosmetic: "pancake makeup." To bring an aircraft to a "pancake landing," i.e., to drop flat to the ground from a low altitude as an emergency measure. The food also is called "griddlecake," "flannel cake," "flapjack" and "hotcake," which last in plural form is to quick sales as "pancake" is to flatness.

pandowdy. A nineteenth-century Americanism, of otherwise unknown origin, for a deep-dish apple pie made with molasses and a thick crust of biscuit dough. Perhaps an inversion of "dowdy pan," as descriptive of the baking vessel and its homely contents. One writer described it in 1893 as "a kind of coarse and broken up apple-pie." In other words, an apple pie in less than apple-pie order.

papaw, a.k.a. **pawpaw.** The custard apple; the fruit of the lower North American tree *Asimina triloba.* The word is probably from the Spanish PAPAYA, with which the pawpaw often has been confused.

papaya. The fruit of the tropical American evergreen tree *Carica papaya.* Spanish from Cariban. See also PAPAW.

paprika. Hungarian via Serbian from Greek *peperi* ("pepper"). Although not introduced into Hungary until the nineteenth century, paprika soon became emblematic of Hungarian cookery, and Hungarian paprika generally is considered the standard of quality throughout the world. According to a popular Hungarian proverb, "One man may yearn for fame, another for wealth, but everyone yearns for paprika *gulyas.*"

paprikash, chicken. From the Hungarian *paprikás czirke,* denotative of the dish's two essential ingredients.

parfait. French "perfect."

Paris-Brest. A popular French filled pastry ring, inspired by and named for a bicycle race between the eponymous cities. Created in 1891, in a pastry shop beside the race route, the cake supposedly was shaped in replication of a biker's tire.

Parker House roll. Named during the late nineteenth century for the Boston hotel where the roll may or may not have originated, but where it certainly was popularized.

Parma ham. Italian *prosciutto di Parma,* a designation strictly regulated by Italian law. See also PROSCIUTTO.

Parmentier, à la. A dedicatory nomenclatural cue in French cookery, signifying a dish made or prominently garnished with potatoes. After Antoine Augustin Parmentier (1737–1813), a military pharmacist and agronomist who successfully promoted potato consumption in France, breaking traditional resistance to the tuber.

parmigiana, alla. See p. xv.

parsley. See p. 122.

parson's nose. The Protestant version of POPE'S NOSE.

partridge. Although heard ad nauseam at Yuletide, the word, given to a confusing number of distinct birds in both hemispheres, doesn't play much of a role in general language. Two varieties of food fish, the golden wrasse and gilt-head bream, are termed "sea partridge," and a certain type of obsolete cannon charge, resembling greatly enlarged bird shot, was called "partridge" in its day.

pashka. A Russian Easter cake decorated with molded reliefs depicting the Passion, and with candied fruits forming the initials *X* and *B* (for *Khristos voskress,* meaning "Christ is risen") in the Cyrillic alphabet. The name of the cake ultimately derives from the Hebrew *Pesach* (Passover), which has been incorporated into the Romance languages (e.g., the Italian Pasqua, the Spanish Pascu de Resurección, the French Pâques) and in the English adjective "paschal."

passion fruit. So termed not for its sexiness but because the blossoms of its sources (chiefly American vines of the genus *Passiflora*) are thought to resemble symbols of the Passion of Jesus, or Stations of the Cross.

pasta. Italian "paste."

pastis. 1. The generic term for a French apéritif flavored with anise seed. "Pernod," in widespread use generically by Americans in Paris, is a brand name for the liquor. *Pastis* is a Provençal dialect word meaning "confused" or "mixed," in reference to the drink's cloudy appearance when it's customarily diluted with water. (In Provence, the brand of overwhelming choice is Ricard.) The liquor is the relatively benign offspring of absinthe, a narcotic substance banned by French law in 1915. **2.** Any of several pastries of southwestern France, the word in this sense having derived from PÂTÉ ("pie").

pâté. Literally "pie" in French (or "paste" without the acute accent). Properly, a pâté is a terrine baked in a pastry crust, but the terms often are used interchangeably.

pawpaw. See PAPAW.

pea. The leguminous seed of the annual vine *Pisum sativum*, invariably invoked plurally in the simile for indistinguishable likeness. Not etymologically akin to "pea jacket" or "peacock."

pea bean. The smallest of the dried white beans.

pea-brained. Intellectually deficient.

pea shooter. A child's blowgun charged with dried split peas.

pea soup. A dense fog.

peach. From the Latin *persicum* (*malum*), "Persian melon" (the fruit is native to China but arrived in Europe via Persia; the modern "Persian melon," *Cumis melo inodorus,* is an unrelated fruit). A term of admiration, as in "a peach of a girl."

peaches-and-cream. See p. 62.

peach Melba. A dessert created during the Belle Epoque by the French master chef Escoffier and named for the Australian soprano Dame Nellie Melba. See also p. xii.

peanut. Neither a pea nor a nut but the seed of the vine *Arachis hypogaea,* native to tropical America. The peanut burrows underground as it matures, hence the name "groundnut" in British English. A small or insignificant person. In plural form, an insignificant amount of money, as in "It's selling for peanuts."

peanut butter. Used in similes for mouth-clogging substances or sticky thicknesses. Occasionally termed "monkey butter" in World War II mess hall slang.

pear-shaped. An adjective for some women's breasts (see p. 60) and the full, round tones of accomplished speakers or singers.

penuche. From Mexican Spanish *panocha,* a diminutive of "bread," from the loaf of raw or brown sugar used in making the fudgelike candy.

pepper. To pelt or shower with small missiles. To enliven speech with colorful tropes, cusswords, etc.

pepper-and-salt. Variant of "salt-and-pepper" (see p. 62).

peppercorn. Price of the Trinity Church Charter, 1697: one.

pepper pot. A.k.a. "Philadelphia pepper pot." A euphemistic name for a tripe soup supposedly improvised during the winter of 1777–78 by a Continental Army cook from Philadelphia. See also TRIPE.

Pernod. See PASTIS.

persimmon. Native to North America but widely thought to be indigenous to Japan, where it was introduced by Commodore Perry in 1855, the fruits of various trees of the genus *Diospyros* take their collective name from an Algonquian term akin to the Cree *pasiminan* ("dried fruit"). Lacking his more experienced friend Pocahontas's native smarts, the Virginia colonist John Smith bit into an unripe persimmon and ruefully concluded that the fruit "will draw a mans mouth awrie."

pesto. A raw or slightly warmed sauce originated in Genoa and compounded by pulverizing its ingredients (saliently including basil) with a pestle (Italian *pestello*), whence the name.

petit four. French "low oven," for the mild temperature at which small, elaborately decorated cakes of this type were baked in the eighteenth century.

pfeffernuesse. Literally "pepper nut," a German cookie traditionally baked at Christmas. Similar cookies are baked elsewhere in northern Europe, under such cognates as the Norwegian *pepperkaker*, Swedish *pepparnotter* and Danish *pebernodder*.

phyllo. Greek "leaf," for the pastry's thinness.

picalilli. Possibly a portmanteau word combining "pickle" and "chile," since the pickled vegetable relish usually contains capsicum peppers.

pickerel. From the Middle English *pikerel,* diminutive of "pike." In Britain, a young pike. In America, any of the smaller species of pike.

pickle. From the Middle Dutch *pekel* via Middle English *pekille.* Possibly after a fourteenth-century Dutch fisherman named Beukelz, popularly credited with the invention of the pickling process, which antedated him by at least a couple of millennia in Egypt and Greece, may have originated as far back as the Paleolithic era and certainly was in extensive use during the early T'ang period (ca. A.D. 618) in China. **1.** An inconvenient situation, a tight spot. **2.** To treat metal with a chemical solution. **3.** To bleach wood, as a floor, with diluted white paint or stain.

pickled. Drunk, smashed.

picklepuss. A sour-faced killjoy.

picnic. A pleasurable or easy activity, a piece of cake. Often used negatively, as in "This job's no picnic." Also the locus of unwanted invaders, as in the simile "as welcome as ants at a ———."

pie. Possibly from the Middle English *pie* or *pye,* diminutive of "magpie," because the pastry, originally filled with miscellaneous edibles, was thought to resemble the acquisitive bird's nest, similarly filled with scrounged materials.

pieds et paquets. French "feet and packets." A Provençal specialty of stuffed sheep's tripe (the "packets") simmered in wine and stock with bacon and sheep's feet.

pierogi, pirozhki. Respectively, a semicircular Polish noodle dumpling filled with meat, cheese, vegetables or any combination thereof, and a Russian savory of filled pastry dough. Both from the Russian *pirozhok*, a diminutive of *pirog*, a larger such pastry.

pig's bones. An expression, used contemptuously by immigrant Chinese in the New York City garment industry, for intricate piece-work that entails more labor than it's worth. Conversely, "soy sauce chicken" is easy, relatively well paying work.

pilaf, pilau, pilaw. Via Turkish and Persian from Osmanli *pilav* ("rice porridge").

piña colada. Spanish for "strained pineapple." *Colada* and the English "colander" both are rooted in the Latin *cōlum* ("sieve" or "filter").

pineapple. See p. 116.

pinto bean. The Spanish *pinto* (also applied to a piebald horse) means "painted." The bean is so named for its mottled seeds.

pistachio. A yellow-green tint. From the color of the nutmeat.

pizza. When the moon hits your eye like a big pizza pie, that's redundant. In modern Italian usage, *pizza* is synonymous with the English "pie."

pluck. The heart, spleen, liver, windpipe and lungs of a meat animal. Courage in the face of difficulties, guts.

plum. A job or assignment coveted for its disproportionate profitability or subsidiary rewards. A dark-purple to deep-reddish color. Formerly, a raisin in a pudding, cake, etc. The "plum" that Little Jack Horner pulled from his pie probably was a raisin.

poach. From the French *pocher* ("to pocket"), meaning to envelop the yolks of eggs in their whites. By extension, to cook any food in simmering liquid.

poblano. The chile takes its name from the Mexican city of Puebla, the birthplace of *mole poblano*, the well-known sauce in which dried *poblanos* or *anchos* play leading roles, along with unsweetened chocolate.

polenta. Italian from Latin *puls* and possibly the earlier Greek *poltos* ("porridge"). The direct culinary ancestor of *polenta* was *pulmentum*, a grain paste on which the Roman legions largely subsisted.

pomegranate. See p. 14.

pomelo. From the Dutch *pompelmoes* ("grapefruit"), whence the French *pamplemousse*. A.k.a. "shaddock," for a Captain Shaddock of the British East India Company, who brought seeds of the tree *Citrus maxima* from Malaysia to Jamaica in 1696. The large fruit of this tree is thought to be the ancestral grapefruit.

pommes Anna. The popular French potato dish was named for Anna Deslions, a woman of fashion during the Second Empire.

pomme, pomme de terre. See pp. 13–14.

pompano. Any of several warm-water marine fishes of the genus

Trachinotus, especially *T. carolinus,* described by Mark Twain as "one of the more delectable forms of sin." From the Spanish *pampano,* a word that somewhat puzzlingly denotes not only the fish but a vine tendril.

poor boy, po' boy. See HERO SANDWICH.

pope's nose. The rump of a cooked fowl, also termed PARSON'S NOSE.

porcino. Italian "little pig" (plural *porcini*), the mushroom *Boletus edulis,* given its popular name for its plumpness. The French *cèpe.*

pork. The infinitely kinky Marquis de Sade may have been the only person ever to use it as a term of endearment, addressing his much-abused wife as "fresh pork of my thoughts." Funds, appointments or other perks wangled by a legislator for his constituency; the benefits of a "pork barrel" arrangement.

   pork pie. A man's snap-brim hat having a low, flat crown.

   porky. Overweight. A nickname or term of address for a tubby individual.

porridge. From Middle English *porray* ("pottage"). A thick cereal, usually of oatmeal.

porter. A dark beer, formerly termed "porter's beer," once favored by porters and other laborers.

porterhouse, porterhouse steak. A cut of beef from the thick end of the short loin, so called for its popularity in nineteenth-century porterhouses: pubs where PORTER was the wetness of choice.

pot. 1. The contentious cooking vessel that calls the kettle black. **2.** A rounded, protuberant stomach, a "pot belly." **3.** A large drinking vessel, a tankard. **4.** The stake or kitty in a card game, as in "feed the pot" or "sweeten the pot." **5.** Marijuana. **6.** A trap for fish or crustaceans. **7.** A toilet bowl. **8.** A communal fund, maintained by members of a social group and used to finance future activities or purchases. **9.** To shoot game for food, rather than sport.

potboiler. A piece of literature or art produced with little regard to quality, in order to realize a quick financial return.

poteen. Illicitly distilled Irish whiskey, from Irish Gaelic *poitīn* ("small pot").

pot, go to. Deteriorate.

pothole. A hole in the ground, especially in a road.

pothouse. Chiefly British. A tavern.

potluck. Whatever food is available for unexpected guests. By extension, any improvisatory solution to a problem.

potshot. An easy shot taken without regard to sporting conventions, simply to put food in a pot. An attack on a sitting duck.

potato. See p. 13.

pot-au-feu. French for "pot on the fire." Defined by Octave Mirabeau as "the fountain of empires." One of the basic dishes of French cookery, descended from the perpetually simmering cauldrons of Medieval northern Europe, to which various ingredients were added as they came to hand, and which were removed from the fire, emptied and cleaned only for Lent. Its counterparts include the *cocido* of Spain, Italy's *bollito misto* ("mixed boil") and the New England boiled dinner. Traditionally served in successive courses of broth, bone marrow on toast and, as the pièce de résistance, sliced meats and vegetables.

pot stickers. Small Chinese wontons, browned on one side, then simmered in broth. So termed for their tendency to adhere to the wok if not watchfully fried.

poularde, poulet, poussin. French for, respectively, a fat roasting hen, a spring chicken and a very young chicken. All three are used as terms of affection and are akin to the English "poultry," from Middle English *pultrie*.

> Said Potiphar's wife, feeling sultry,
> "Hey, Joseph, let's do some adultery."
> Said Joe to P's wife,
> "Lady, not on your life.
> "You're some chicken, but not kosher pultrie."

pound cake. So called because early recipes called for a pound each of its chief ingredients.

pretzel. In similes, anything twisted out of shape. In Medieval monasteries, pretzels were served to young scholars, to remind them of arms crossed in prayer.

prosciutto. Although simply the generic Italian noun meaning "ham" of any sort, cured or fresh, the term is generally understood, in Italy and elsewhere, to mean the air- and salt-cured hams of Parma and San Danieli. See also PARMA HAM.

prune. A sour-natured individual, a killjoy.

prune-faced. Excessively wrinkled.

pudding. What the proof of is in the eating. The penis (see p. 61.)

pullet. Middle English *polet, pulet* from Old French *poulet* and, ultimately, the Latin *pullus*, the young of an animal or fowl. According to the West Coast newspaper columnist Jack Smith, a "pullet surprise" was a child's mishearing of "Pulitzer Prize." See also POULARDE, POULET, POUSSIN.

pumpernickel. German from Early High German *Pumpern* ("a fart") and *Nickel* ("devil"), so termed for its supposed tendency to induce flatulence.

pumpkin. A term of endearment, sometimes with "pie."

pumpkinseed. A North American sunfish, *Lepomis gibbosus*.

Q

quahog. See LITTLENECK CLAM.

quiche. French from German *Küchen* ("cake"). What real men don't eat.

quince. Ultimately from the Greek Kudōnia ("Cydonia," the ancient name for Canea, the fruit's supposed birthplace). A symbol of love to the Romans, presented to one's intended as a token of engagement.

R

radish. From the Latin *rādix* ("root").

ragout. From the French *ragoûter*, to revive the appetite.

raisin. See PLUM.

rancid. Latin *rancidus* from *rancēre* ("to stink"). Applied figuratively to anything or anyone unsavory.

rape. The Eurasian plant *Brassicus rapus*, also called broccoli raab, broccoli (or brocoletti) di rape, Chinese flowering cabbage, etc., when eaten as a vegetable, but cultivated chiefly for its oil-bearing seeds (see CANOLA OIL) and as animal fodder. From the Latin *rāpa*, *rāpum* ("turnip").

raspberry. The Bronx cheer. A color resembling that of raspberries.

raspberry kidney. A human kidney of morbid granular structure.

raspberry lid. An affliction of the eyelid producing a granular texture.

ravioli. According to most reference works consulted, the singular form is *raviolo*, from a dialectical diminutive for "turnip," derived from the Latin *rāpa*. Although ravioli can be filled with any vegetable, meat or cheese, singly or in combination, there seem to be no regional versions of the pasta dumplings in which turnips play a role significant enough to validate the attribution. More convincing is Waverley Root's contention that until the early nineteenth century the noun was *rabioli*, "a Genoese dialect word meaning things of little value—rubbish, say, or, in the kitchen, leftovers."

razor clam. So called for its resemblance to a closed straight razor (and perhaps the sharpness of its valve edges).

red, a bowl of. A portion of chili con carne, particularly in Texas.

red-eye gravy. Perhaps so called because hot coffee, conducive to sleeplessness, is an ingredient of most versions.

refried beans. *Frijoles refritos,* a misnomer in both English and Spanish. The beans in question are fried only once after previously having been cooked in water.

rémoulade. French from the Picard dialect *ramolas,* "horseradish," although horseradish isn't an ingredient of the sauce in either its original French or Louisiana Creole treatments. Go figure.

restaurant. "Restorative" in French, from *restaurer,* "to restore." The term was applied to an eating establishment for the first time in 1765, when a Parisian shopkeeper hung a sign over his door proclaiming that "Boulanger sells magical restoratives." The advertiser was misnamed; he was a soup vendor, but a *boulanger* is a baker.

Reuben sandwich. Named for its putative creator, Arthur Reuben, the owner of a New York City deli.

rhubarb. Also called "pie plant." A heated argument, hassle or melee.

rickey, gin rickey, lime rickey. A tall drink of club soda, liquor (usually gin) and lime juice. Probably after an otherwise unidentified Colonel Rickey.

> Now, this one is just a bit tricky:
> A Hibernian toper named Hickey
>   Hid a verse in his gin
>   And then, with a grin,
> He named his creation Lime Rickey.

rijsttafel. Dutch "rice table," an Indonesian buffet of cooked rice accompanied by myriad side dishes, sweet and savory, used as garnishes throughout the meal.

risotto. Italian "rice." The grain staple or a dish thereof, usually garnished with vegetables or seafoods. Lately, some food writers wrongheadedly have taken to terming various riceless dishes *risotti*, as in "barley risotto."

roast. Middle English *rosten* from Old French *rostir*, probably from Old High German *rōsten*, from *Rōst* ("grate" or "gridiron"). **1.** To heat ore in a furnace. **2.** To criticize harshly or ridicule unmercifully but good-naturedly. **3.** An often raucous ceremony, peculiar to show business, at which the guest of honor's foibles are exposed, his shtick lampooned, etc.

Rocky Mountain oyster. See MOUNTAIN OYSTER.

rollmops. A marinated herring fillet wrapped around a gherkin or pickled onion. From the German *rollen* ("to roll") and *Mops* ("pug dog"), probably from a perceived resemblance to the latter.

romaine or Cos lettuce. Depends on whether you choose to believe it's of Roman origin or first was cultivated on the Aegean island of Cos.

rutabaga. Dialectical Swedish *rotabagge* ("baggy root"). Also called "swede."

S

sabra. A native Israeli. The Hebrew for "prickly pear." From the widespread Israeli perception that natives of that country, like the fruits of various cacti of the genus *Opuntia*, are sweet-natured beneath a forbidding exterior.

saccharine. Cloyingly sweet, often in an affected manner, as in "saccharine smile."

sachertorte. Named for the rich chocolate layer cake's nineteenth-century creator, Franz Sacher.

safflower oil. A cooking oil pressed from the seeds of the plant *Carthamus tinctorius*, native to Asia and having orange flowers that yield an extensively used dyestuff. A.k.a. "saffron thistle," from its coloristic resemblance to true SAFFRON.

saffron. The dried stigmas of the Old World plant *Crocus sativus*, used as a spice, food colorant and dyestuff. A yellow color favored by Asiatic ascetics and such Western converts as Moonies and Hare Krishnas.

sage. Derived from the Latin *salvia* ("the healing plant"), from *salvus* ("healthy," "safe"). See also p. 43.

Saint-Honoré, gateau. An elaborate French cake, topped with a ring of caramelized cream puffs, with a cream-based filling at its center. The eponymous honoree (oops!) is the patron saint of pastry cooks.

St. John's bread. Carob, a seed pod used in powdered form as a chocolate substitute. Also known as "locust bean," the connection with the preacher-saint stemming from his diet of honey and locusts.

salad. See p. 43.

> **salad days.** The youthful, inexperienced years of one's life, as in Shakespeare's "my salad days, when I was green in judgment."

salami. Italian "salted (pork)" from the Latin *sal* ("salt"). See also p. 43.

Salisbury steak. Named for the nineteenth-century English nutritionist J. H. Salisbury, who advocated liberal consumption of beef as a health measure. How times have changed!

Sally Lunn. According to the relatively taciturn American Heritage Dictionary, "A muffinlike tea cake (Supposedly invented by Sally Lunn, 18th-century English baker)." The somewhat more expansive E. S. Dallas has this to say:

> *Sally Lunn is an honoured name from the Land's End to John o' Groats. But why should the reader be called upon to meditate upon her virtues in these pages, in which so little has been said about the Bath bun, the Banbury cake, the Scotch shortbread, the Brioche, the Baba, the Savarin,*

the Gauffre, and many another noble thing? The reason
is that her name has been mixed up with a little culinary
scandal; and it is necessary to vindicate her fair fame. The
greatest cook of modern times, Carême, came over to Eng-
land to minister to the palate of the Prince Regent. He
did not stay long, but he stayed long enough to appreciate
the charms of Sally Lunn and her ever memorable cake.

On his return to France, according to Dallas, Carême rechristened the cake *solilemne*. It's still popular among the French, who now term it *solilemme* or *solilem* on menus that also may feature *bifteck* and *rosbif.*

salsify. See OYSTER PLANT.

salt. See p. 43.

saltimbocca. Italian "jump in the mouth," a Roman dish of veal, prosciutto and sage, for the appetency excited in those who are served the dish.

samovar. A Russian tea urn. From *samo* ("self") and *varit* ("to boil"), i.e., "self-boiling."

samphire. The succulent shore herb *Crithmum maritimum*, variously known in France as *perce-pierre, pousse-pierre, casse-pierre* and *bacile*, the *-pierre* suffixes having to do with the plant's propensity for sprouting on rocky ground.

sandwich. The derivation from the eponymous English earl is too well known to merit further discussion here.

sangria. The fruit-based wine punch (often laced with brandy) takes its name from the Spanish *sangre* ("blood"), for its color.

sardine. Probably from the Greek Sardo (Sardinia), the immature herring's principal source of export in the ancient world.

sauce. Ultimately from the Latin *sal* ("salt"). See also p. 43. Generically, booze. Sauciness, impudence. To add piquancy to. Soft soap, ameliorative speech. What's fit for the gander if fit for the goose.

sauerkraut. German "sour cabbage."

satire. From Old French *satira, satura* ("mixed fruits"), with the implication of satiety.

savory. Either of two Old World aromatic herbs, *Satureja hortensis* or *S. montana*, respectively, summer and winter savory. Any food characterized by appetizing flavors, not including sweetness. Morally inoffensive or respectable, usually used negatively, as in "an unsavory character."

scallion. From the Latin *Ascalonia caepa* ("onion of Ascalon"). "Rapscallion" is etymologically unrelated. See also SHALLOT.

scallop. Middle English *scalop* from Old French *escalope* ("shell").

scaloppine. Italian plural of *scaloppina*, diminutive of *scaloppa*, a thin cut of meat curled, when cooked, like a shell.

scampi. The Italian plural of *scampo*, a type of prawn. The menu term "shrimp scampi" is a solecism meaning shrimp prepared in the manner of prawns, i.e., broiled with garlic and butter or olive oil.

Schlag. German "whipped cream."

schmaltz, schmalz. Yiddish for rendered chicken fat. Sentimentality, corniness.

schmear. A smear of spreadable food, as cream cheese. Yiddish-derived New York deli patois (e.g., "a bagel with a schmear").

schnapps. From Low German *Snaps,* "mouthful" or "dram."

schnitzel. German "cutlet."

schnitzel, wiener. A breaded veal cutlet prepared in the style of Vienna.

Scotch woodcock. A wishful euphemism for a British dish of toast spread with anchovy paste and scrambled egg.

scrapple. Pennsylvania Dutch diminutive of "scrap," a type of sausage made with cornmeal.

scungilli. See CONCH.

Seckel pear. Named for an eighteenth-century Pennsylvania farmer.

seltzer. Garbled form of "Niederselters," a western German town known for its mineral water.

shaddock. See POMELO.

shallot. Like "SCALLION," the word derives from the Latin *Ascalonia caepa*, after the Palestinian city of Ascalon, where the onion family member was thought to have originated.

sherbet; sorbet. Via Turkish and Persian from the Arabic *shariba* ("to drink"). In Britain, "sherbet" is a diluted, sweetened fruit juice.

sherry. See p. 96.

shoofly pie. So called because its sweetness attracts flies that must be shooed away.

shrimp. A diminutive or insignificant person.

simmer. To be filled with barely controllable anger. With "down," to calm oneself after blowing one's stack.

sirloin. Although the English term is from the French *sur longe* (p. 47), the cut of beef is called *aloyau* in France.

skewer. To stab with a cutting remark or clear evidence of guilt, as to put a piece of meat on a spit.

skoal. The Scandinavian toast translates literally as "drinking cup" but derives from the Old Norse *skalle* ("skull"), skulls of slain enemies having been used as drinking vessels by ancient Norsemen.

smörgasbord. Swedish "bread and butter table," from Old Norse *smor* ("fat") *gas* ("goose") and *bordh* ("table"), with cognates in other Scandinavian languages. Any large, varied array offering a multiplicity of temptations, as in "The Big Apple is a smörgasbord of entertainment."

snickerdoodle. The cookie originated in New England during the nineteenth century. Its name has no known derivation.

sole. Any of various flatfishes of the family Soleidae. Called *solea Jovi* ("Jupiter's sandal") in ancient Rome, for its shape.

sommelier. A supercilious wine steward might be taken down a peg or two if reminded that his French title derives from the term *bête de somme*: "beast of burden."

soup. A troublesome situation, as in "He's in the soup now." Any liquefied mixture, as thin slush or mud.

sourdough. A nineteenth-century settler or prospector, especially in Alaska or northwestern Canada, so termed for his bread of choice.

spare ribs. Called *cartouchières* ("cartridge belts") in French butchers' slang, from the appearance of the racks.

spice. To add zest or piquancy, as to a story.

spick-and-span. The expression "span-new" dates from around 1300, when freshly cut wooden chips were used as *spans* (later, "spoons"). "Spick" was coupled with "span" in the sixteenth century, possibly with reference to the spike used to impale meat.

spinach. Folding money.

  spinach, facial. Whiskers.

spring roll. So termed because the filled pastry appetizers traditionally are eaten in China and Vietnam at the New Year, which occurs in early spring.

steak tartare, tartar steak. So called for the Tatars (or Tartars), the Mongolian people who supposedly subsisted largely on scraped raw meat tenderized beneath their horsemen's saddles. Recently, such terms as "tuna tartare" idiotically have been incorporated into menu terminology.

stew. Middle English *stewen,* "to bathe in hot water or steam," ultimately from the Greek *tuphos* ("smoke" or "vapor"). **1.** To swelter in humid heat. **2.** To worry, experience anxiety. A state of worry or anxiety; mental or emotional agitation. **3.** A chronic lush. **4.** An archaic term, usually pluralized, for a whorehouse. **5.** An airline attendant (not of the same derivation; see p. 56.)

stewed. Smashed, bombed, soused, three sheets to the wind.

stew in one's own juice. Undergo problems of one's own making, sweat out a self-imposed difficulty.

stockfish. A wood-hard (we're talking hardwood here) air-dried fish, such as cod or haddock, softened in water before use. From the German *Stock* ("stick") and *Fisch* ("fish"). Rabelais termed it *stocficz* in *Pantagruel,* and the current Italian word is *stoccafissa.*

succotash. From Narragansett *miskquatash* ("boiled corn kernels").

sugar. Money. A term of endearment. To make more appealing (usually with "coat").

sugar daddy. A man who keeps and spends money on a woman, who is (usually) younger than he.

sugar-head. Moonshine whiskey.

sugar hill. A brothel district in an African American neighborhood.

sugar report. A letter from a sweetheart to a World War II serviceman.

sukiyaki. Japanese. Literally "grilled on a plowshare." A dish originated by peasants who prepared it surreptitiously in the fields, in violation of dietary taboos against meat or fowl. Termed "friendship dish" in modern Japan, for its appeal to outlanders.

sunchoke. The Jerusalem artichoke. See p. 9.

sundae. Origin uncertain but possibly coined to dissociate connotations or pleasurable indulgence in the dish from the Christian sabbath, when it usually was eaten.

swede. See RUTABAGA.

sweeten. To make anything, as a business offer or poker pot, more palatable or potentially profitable.

sweet potato. The ocarina, a simple hollow clay wind instrument with rudimentary stops.

symposium. Latin from Greek *sumposion* ("drinking party"). Originally the continuation of a formal dinner or banquet, a course following the meal proper, designed to stimulate thirst and discussion.

T

Tabasco. Literally "moist earth." A pungent chile, *Capsicum frutescens*, named for the Mexican state of its supposed origin. The trademark of the hot sauce produced since the mid-nineteenth century by the McIlhenny family of Avery Island, Louisiana.

table setter. See p. 66.

taco. Mexican Spanish from Spanish "wad," "pad."

tamale, hot. See p. 58.

tangelo. The hybrid citrus fruit takes its portmanteau name from "tangerine" and "POMELO."

tapas. An assortment of Spanish hors d'oeuvre. From *tapa* ("lid," "cover"). Originally a small saucer balanced atop a wine bottle to keep flies from drowning happily in the plonk. At some point, it occurred to someone (probably a tavern owner or bartender) to serve morsels of food on the saucers, thereby initiating a custom now almost religiously observed in Spain, during the early-evening hours before dinner, when people drift from *tasca* (saloon) to *tasca* sampling *tapas*. If the *tapas* kept the flies out of the wine, what kept the flies off the *tapas?*

tapenade. A Provençal condiment, often served as an appetizer, of capers, blanched anchovies and pitted black olives, augmented in some versions by various herbs and savories, notably tuna. The French counterpart of the earlier Italian *caponata*.

taramasalata. From the Greek *tarama* ("carp roe") and *salata* ("salad").

tarte Tatin. A French upside-down apple tart that originated, according to legend, when a pair of spinster sisters named Tatin executed a klutzy *pas de deux* during which the dessert landed flipside-up on their kitchen floor and then frugally was served as though the inversion had been deliberate.

tempura. Japanese "fried food." The cooking technique itself was introduced to Japan by the Portuguese.

terrine. A naked PÂTÉ usually served from the baking dish of the same name.

thousand-year egg. An even more hyperbolic designation for the so-called hundred-year-old egg of Chinese cookery. See p. 88.

toad-in-the-hole. A whimsically named British dish of link sausages wrapped in Yorkshire pudding batter. The antecedent of the American pig-in-the-blanket.

toast. As a drinking salute, the term stems from an Old World custom of placing a slice of toasted bread, to be eaten by the guest of honor, in a communal goblet of hot spiced wine.

Toll House cookie. The original chocolate chip cookie, created during the 1930s at the Toll House restaurant, near Whitman, Massachusetts.

tomalley. The liver of a lobster, considered a delicacy by those who aren't put off by green slime. From the Carib for "lobster [or crab] liver sauce."

tomato. See pp. 15, 57.

tortellini. Italian derivative of *torta* ("tart"). A savory-filled ring-shaped pasta dumpling, supposedly modeled on the female navel, more specifically the umbilicus of Venus. According to the otherwise reliable Waverley Root, accomplished tortellini makers, invariably women recognizable by the "sweat around the[ir] haunches," are capable of producing upward of six thousand tortellini per hour by hand—a patent impossibility, however sweaty their haunches may get. Tortellini machines can turn out ten times that volume with no sweat. Tortelli, tortelletti, tortelloni, etc., are variants named according to size.

tortilla. In Mexican Spanish, the basic national bread, made with unleavened corn (*masa*) or wheat flour and baked on a griddle in the form of a very thin pancake. In Spain, an omelet.

tortoni. An ice cream popularized in the late eighteenth century in Paris, by an expatriate Italian restaurateur of that name, the successor to one Velloni.

tournedos. Sliced tenderloin of beef, so called for the butchers' stalls in the Paris market Les Halles (now defunct), which turned their backs (*tournant le dos*) on the fresh fish department.

treacle. Anything cloyingly sweet.

tripe. Nonsense, rubbish, crap. See also p. 100.

trivet. Old English *trefet* from the Latin *tripēs* ("three-footed").

truffle. By way of various Medieval languages from the Latin *tūber*.

truffle, chocolate. So called for its richness, shape, color and, in early cocoa-dusted versions, its close resemblance to the subterranean fungus.

trumpet of death. So termed for its shape and lugubrious color, the wild mushroom more appetizingly is known as "horn of plenty."

tunafish. See p. 51.

turkey. A theatrical floperoo. A dupe or loser. See also p. 91.

turkey, Mississippi. A North American freshwater fish of the genus *Ictiochus,* more formally called "buffalo fish" for its humped back.

turkey, talk. Get down to brass tacks.

turkey trot. A ragtime dance imitative of a running turkey's movements.

turnip. What you can't get blood out of.

turnspit. A dog bred specifically to rotate a gear-operated roasting spit by running on a treadmill. The breed of such dogs.

tutti-frutti. Italian "all fruits."

U

ullage. Peripatetically from the French *oeil* ("eye," "bunghole"), derived from the Latin *oculus* ("eye"). The quantity of wine lost in the barrel or bottle through evaporation or leakage, measured by the vacant space left between the contents' surface and the stopper.

V

vanilla. Colorless or bland, as in "a vanilla personality." See pp. 101–02.

variety meat(s). See OFFAL.

venison. The word goes back to the Latin *vēnāri*, "to hunt (game)," as do "venery" (hunting) and "venerial" (of or pertaining to hunting) but not "venery," as in the pursuit of sexual pleasure, or "venereal" in the sexual sense, both from *venus*. To pursue a deer is venerial, but to chase a dear is venereal.

> Carniverous Alfred Lord Tennyson
> Offered a prandial benison:
> "O blest be this bread,"
> Lord Tennyson said,
> "And more so this saddle of venison."

vermicelli. Italian "little worms." Do resentful kids in Italy threaten to "go out and eat *vermicelli*?"

vermouth. From the German *Wermut* ("wormwood"), a former ingredient of the aromatic wine and, earlier, absinthe.

vinegar. From the French *vin aigre* ("sour wine").

vinegar, piss and. A term denoting feistiness, as in "full of piss and vinegar."

vodka. Russian diminutive of *voda* ("water").

W

waffle. To equivocate, particularly on a political issue.

Waldorf salad. Named for its creation, at New York City's Waldorf Hotel, by the celebrated headwaiter Oscar Tshirky, known as "Oscar of the Waldorf."

whiskey, whisky. Respectively, the American and British spellings of the word derived via *usquebaugh* from the Irish Gaelic *uisce beathad* ("water of life").

whiskey blossom. Rubescence of the facial skin, caused by ruptured capillaries and attributed to heavy drinking.

whiskey jack. The Canada jay, *Periscoreus canadensis,* from an obsolete folk term, "whiskey John," derived from the Cree *wisican(is)*: "gray jay."

X

X-rated fortune cookie. A fortune cookie with a racy message, such as "Lady pilot who flies upside-down has crack up."

Y

yakitori. Japanese *yaki* ("grilled") and *tori* ("fowl").

yam. See p. 12.

Yankee. See p. 49.

yolk. From Old English *geoloca,* from *geolu* ("yellow").

Z

zabaglione. From the Neapolitan dialect word *zapillare* ("to foam") whence, indirectly, the French *sabayon.*

zakuski. Russian hors d'oeuvre. A diminutive plural noun derived from a verb meaning "to nibble."

zampone. A boned pig's trotter stuffed with forcemeat. From the Italian *zampa* ("paw").

zingara, alla. Italian "gypsy woman's–style."

zuppa inglese. Italian "English soup." A dessert based on the English "trifle," something of little importance.

zwieback. German "twice-baked."

Bibliography

Bastianich, Lidia, and Jay Jacobs. *La Cucina di Lidia.* Doubleday, 1990.

Chang, K. C., ed. *Food in Chinese Culture.* Yale University Press, 1977.

Dallas, E. S. *Kettner's Book of the Table.* Centaur Press, 1968.

Dickson, Paul. *Dickson's Word Treasury.* John Wiley & Sons, 1992.

Elkort, Martin. *The Secret Life of Food.* Jeremy P. Tarcher, 1991.

Funk, Charles Earl. *A Hog on Ice and Other Curious Expressions.* Harper & Brothers, 1948.

Garrison, Webb. *Why You Say It.* Rutledge Hill Press, 1992.

Herbst, Sharon Tyler. *Food Lover's Companion.* Barron's, 1990.

Jacobs, Jay. *Gastronomy.* Newsweek Books, 1975.

Lang, Jennifer Harvey, ed. *Larousse Gastronomique.* Crown, 1988.

Lewin, Esther, and Albert E. Lewin. *The Thesaurus of Slang.* Facts on File, 1988.

Naj, Amal. *Peppers.* Alfred A. Knopf, 1992.

Root, Waverley. *Food.* Simon and Schuster, 1980.

Root, Waverley. *The Food of Italy.* Atheneum, 1971.

Rosengarten, Frederic, Jr. *The Book of Spices.* Pyramid Books, 1973.

Scharfenberg, Horst. *The Cuisines of Germany.* Poseidon Press, 1989.

Schneider, Elizabeth. *Uncommon Fruits and Vegetables.* Harper & Row, 1986.

Simeti, Mary Taylor. *Pomp and Sustenance.* Alfred A. Knopf, 1989.

Tannahill, Reay. *Food in History.* Stein and Day, 1973.

Trager, James. *The Food Book.* Avon Books, 1970.

Visser, Margaret. *The Rituals of Dinner.* Penguin Books, 1992.

Wentworth, Harold, and Stuart Flexner Berg. *Dictionary of American Slang.* Crowell, 1975.

Index